Brothers of the Sun
the
Pagan Men's Mysteries

By Reverend Terry Riley

Heka House Publishing
Memphis, USA
2011

1

FIRST EDITION, 2011

Cover design by Sonya Miller
Editing and book design by Sonya Miller

Library of Congress Cataloging-in-Publication Data,
Riley, Terry.

Brothers of the sun: the pagan men's mysteries/Rev. Terry
Riley.
    p.   cm.
Includes bibliographical references and index.
ISBN 1461017998
1. Body/Mind and Spirit   2. Magickal Studies   I. Title

Heka House publishing does not participate in, endorse, or
have any authority or responsibility concerning private
business transactions between our authors and the public.

All mail addressed to the author is forwarded but the
publisher cannot, unless specifically instructed by the author,
give out an address or phone number.

**Heka House Publishing, 603 Estridge Drive, Memphis,
Tn, 38122**
www.hekahouse.com
Printed in the United States of America

The Virtues of Wisdom are:
"To be aware of all things,
To endure all things,
To be removed from all things"
----Druidic Triad

To Ivy

Blessed Be!

Lovely Lady!

3

Terry Riley

Table of Contents

Acknowledgments

I would like to show my gratitude to all the people who helped make the writing of this book possible.

First the entire Pagan community in which I live. The unity that has developed, over the past eighteen years, has made it possible for us to learn and grow in our own spiritual paths without having to spend a lot of our time wasted on egotistical witch wars.

Then there are certain individuals who pushed me to write this book when I was being lazy, thank you Morgana, Scott Summers, Trudy Herring, David Chadwick, and Dorothy Morrison.

To my Church members for all their patience and support. To the Temple of the Sacred Gift – ATC. To Summerland Grove Church.

To our children, Zachariah and Amberly, for sacrificing time with Mom and Dad. To my loving wife and life partner Amanda.

May the Lord and Lady bless you all!

Terry Michael Riley

FOREWORD

Brothers of the Sun was established in the year 2000 as a weekend retreat for Pagan men to gather together to discuss and learn about men's mysteries in Paganism. It is hosted by the Southern Delta Church of Wicca-ATC annually.

With the popularity of Paganism and Wicca as a religious path in these modern times, many books and information about the supposedly Old Religion have been published and disseminated to the general public. However, since most of the material on the market about the Goddess Religion seems to be primarily geared toward women, as it should be; we feel there is a need for Pagan/Wiccan men to learn about their path within Goddess Religion.

Not much about the male's path or role in Paganism/Wicca is available out there. So the Brothers of the Sun Weekend Retreats were created to help men understand the God/Goddess within them.
During the two-day retreat the aspects of manhood are examined and honored through workshops and sacred rituals.

The focus is mainly upon the triple aspect of the God as the Rove, the Father and the Sage. How these energies express themselves in each man are how they affect us consciously and subconsciously.

It is a great weekend for understanding one's self and communing with the male/female aspect of divinity. 2011 will be our seventh year of Brothers of the Sun. More and more men, who attend each year, are amazed at how fulfilled spiritually and psychologically, they feel after spending the weekend with a group of Pagan/Wiccan men seeking to understand themselves and their own chosen path of spirituality.

Although much has been written about the God of Witchcraft, men within Paganism need a way to help them come to know and understand the God within themselves. That is the intent of this work.

This book has been utilized at our men's gathering as a guide to what the weekend is all about. We decided to publish it so the information could be more readily accessible to men truly seeking this knowledge.

We have designed this work to appeal to men who are new to the path of Paganism, as well as offering information to the advanced practitioner. Rites of Passage are examined and utilized within the context. They were written for coven or group work, but they can be easily adapted for solitary work as well.

Not all of the aspects of manhood are covered in this work. That would take a book the size of a set of encyclopedias. The main focus is on the internal and external growth of men through the different stages of growth throughout life.

Do we have all the answers to men's mysteries? I am sad to say, we do not. I think we do have some worthwhile perspectives to help enlighten one upon their personal path of spirituality. To that end, I dedicate this work.

So Mote it Be!

Reverend Terry Michael Riley

Note: I realize that to some there is a difference, in definition, between Witch, Wicca, and Pagan. I use the words interchangeably in this work to fit the concept of my writing; but they are acknowledged here to mean generalized Paganism.

Introduction: Concepts on Relationships
By: Rev. Amanda Riley

I realize that many women will pick up this book in hopes to understand their Pagan/Wiccan men a little better. However, we cannot understand our men until we better understand ourselves.

Pagan men have some of the same programmed concepts as any other males just as we, women have concepts we were raised with and yet must overcome. Patience, love and understanding is what we all need to learn to work together as male and female instead of against one another.

Terry and I have been married over twenty five years and have had many issues, concepts and ego battles to overcome. We have fought the good fight and learned to work as a team. It has not been easy at times on either of our parts.

I grew up with the idea that I was supposed to be the quiet submissive wife. He is the strong one and I am weak and need him to make my decisions and fight my battles for me. I began our relationship by waiting on him hand and foot. I would not argue or fight with him or stand my ground on anything. What he said went, and that was that! I was 21 years old when we married, he was 31 so of course he was smarter, wiser and older so he knew more than I did or at least that is what I believed.

Shortly into our relationship, he broke my heart, turned my world upside down. He sat me down one evening after I had made sure dinner was on the table when he got home, ran his bath water, laid out his clean clothes, fixed his coffee and fluffed his chair.
He asked me why I was doing all of these things and I calmly stated, "Well, as your wife that is what I am supposed to do." He proceeded to explain to me that he married me to be his equal, to be at his side to help him in his life's path as well as for him to help me by being at my side and helping me with my life's path. He told me he did not marry me to be a slave to his every whim and that he was perfectly capable of fixing his own coffee and running his own bath water. He said he wanted me to think, act and be who I was and not what I thought he wanted me to be.

This certainly shocked me and threw me into a tailspin. I was trained to act and speak like the perfect housewife. So now what was I suppose to do? In my mind I was now useless because he wouldn't let me take proper care of him. He would not tell me how he wanted me to wear my hair, what kind of clothes I should wear, where I could go or what I could do. I was on my own and scared to death that I would make major mistakes.

It took several years of battles within me and many tears to learn how to be a woman, an equal to my husband, someone to share, give, live and love with. Now I look back on it all and can laugh about the many talks we had and the immaturity and insecurities I had been raised with.

When I state my opinion now or make my wishes known sometimes he mutters under his breath, "Why did I ever teach her to think? I had the perfect life and no arguments." Yet he has told me numerous times how much he appreciates the fact that I am his equal. And that I can assume responsibilities and take the load from his shoulders. He does not have to pretend to be my Prince Charming. He can laugh with me, cry with me, yell at me and argue with me and in the end we hug and go on, knowing we are balanced and compliment one another.

I remember another hard lesson I learned in becoming the equal partner in our coven. In 1994, we had a small coven and I was the acting High Priestess. I say acting, because I was not qualified in knowledge, experience or wisdom to run a coven at that level Terry had been running the coven as the High Priest. I finally began to grow and became ready to take my place as

High Priestess not just acting High Priestess. So after much thought, meditation and contemplation I decided it was time to tell Terry I was ready.

I sat him down and stated, "I am ready to take my place as a true High Priestess so you need to call a meeting to let these people know. You should explain to them that as the High Priestess they should respect me and treat me as they do you now that I am ready."

Terry said, "This is my coven, I started it and if you want to be High Priestess you have to take it from me. I will not give it to you."

What a can of worms that opened! We had a long tiring conversation where he explained to me that he could not make these people treat me any such way that I had to earn the respect and love of the coven.

It took me about three years from that point to actually grow into the High Priestess that the coven and Terry needed. Many hours of study, meditation, crying and frustration before I realized that I could do this and that these people actually did respect me for who I am and what I am and not because I was Terry's wife. I had to come into my own so to speak. That was a hard lesson.

Over the past few years I have grown more and more. I have learned people only treat you the way you treat them and that you have to earn respect. It is not given freely.

I know many of you are shocked when you realize you are equal. Many of you are like me, and get scared knowing if you don't depend on a man you might make mistakes. It takes a lot of guts to take the responsibility for your life and to be an equal to your partner. If you want to understand Pagan men especially, look into the deep rooted programming of yourself and them. Watch their parents interact and you will see these concepts and learn how to recognize them in your mate.

Read this book with an open mind and open heart. Look at your mate with love, patience and understanding. Reading one book won't give you all the knowledge you need but it can certainly help.

Go within your deep rooted concepts and do some weeding. Be their equal. We all like challenge and the thrill of the hunt. We are not happy when someone cowers to us, we want them to challenge us and force us to grow. Consciously we may not realize this and get angry when people do challenge our concepts, beliefs or ideas, however if it was not a challenge why would you argue? Learn to recognize your weaknesses and grow from them and most of all recognize your mate's weakness and help him to grow into the man he wants to be, not the man you think you want him to be. Pointing out his weaknesses will not help him it will only cause him to rebel just as you would, instead love him, support him and let him be who he is deep inside.

I Paganism in Modern Times

In the beginning before time was… before life emerged from the abyss, there was loneliness. There from the darkest depths of nothingness… an urge surged!

The Urge to express, to experience, to survive the complete boredom of existence without sustenance.

A mournful wail of frustration echoed throughout the cosmos. This willful vibration stirred the un-manifest to begin to move. That movement spawned a plan of law and Order to govern itself.

Two principles came into being that ruled movement; action with reaction and destruction with regeneration. These two principles created the first Universal Law… the Perpetual Transmutation of Radiant Energy. Nothing could actually be created nor destroyed. It just merely IS.

The idea here is that way back before anything was manifest there was nothing. That's difficult for our finite minds to comprehend; a realm of nothing, no light, no dark, a vast empty void.

All religions refer to a power or a force that existed in that void un-manifested. Science does not acknowledge its existence because they can find no proof of it beyond theory. Science deals with facts. However logical reasoning has to accept that there was "Something" in the void to start all of creation. It has been given many names and many labels by every religion; many Wiccans and Pagans simply call it the All-Spirit.

II Pagan Manhood

What does it mean to be a man? Like most boys that were raised in America, we were taught by our fathers and other men the expression, "Be a man." Usually we were told this when we were hurt, you know a skinned knee or bruised elbow. In their way of thinking, it was meant as a way to toughen us up. Looking back on it now, it did toughen us up, although not physically. We toughened up all right, but in our emotions.

How many men cannot or will not express their deep emotions, except perhaps in anger or frustration? Could it be that the programmed concepts of our childhood planted seeds within us? That tenderness, nurturing and loving emotions were a sign of weakness? Why would this be so? Where did men get the idea that softer expression of their emotions was weak? Have you heard the expression, "Women are the weaker sex?"

If you research history back a few hundred or thousand years, you will find a different outlook on the power of the woman. For instance, the Celtic societies of long ago treated the women as equals to men. They followed the matriarchal lineages because the certainty of the mother was known to all; this is not so with the father. If you will take a quick look at the history of the American Iroquois Nation, you will find the chiefs did not make decisions on the welfare of their people. The decisions were made by the elder women of the moon lodge.

Originally, in Europe, the sun was a feminine symbol. Only because of Roman and Christian influences did the sun become a masculine symbol. But why did men change their concept and begin to suppress the power of the women? The answer is fear.

Around the time of the Industrial Revolution is the time that patriarchy came into being. It was a time of linear thinking, a time of mathematics. This was the power of men, this was their domain. Men had the power of the mind, the power of change! Men did not have the power that women did with their menstrual cycles: women had the power of the blood, the power of creation!

Men have always warred with one another. Trying to out maneuver each other with strategy, fully utilizing their power to change these concepts even filtered their way into the religious systems. Most religions of the matriarchal systems promoted the creative power of the feminine aspect through the symbol of the menstrual blood. Male religious leaders, knowing men could not produce their own blood cycle as women did, became jealous and produced the equivalent effect in the blood sacrifices of animals and humans.

Modern men, because of centuries of programming and deep-seated fears, are completely out of balance with their true masculine nature. The concept of modern man is that he has to be strong and show absolute control of the so-called weaker emotions. He must be capable of taking care of a weak, timid and helpless woman. This is what we classify as the "Prince Charming Syndrome."

Now let's be fair, both men and women of the modern times try very hard to live up to this illusion. The sad thing is that most men and women do not know that it is an illusion. They believe that it is "just the way things are." I believe that the Prince Charming Syndrome has its conceptual roots in the religion of Christianity. Their doctrine says women will be submissive to the men. Now before you accuse me of Christian bashing, hear me out. It has been proven that in time, a culture can assimilate a religious idea or doctrine into its everyday concepts, even if the majority of the people do not practice the religion. Because 5 percent of the people think, 15 percent think they think and the other 80 percent would rather die than think.

This is sad but true. It might lead one to imagine that most people can be compared to merely carbon-based robots letting a society dictate to them what they should think, how they should act and what they should feel. Most ideas of what a man should be have been indoctrinated into our culture by the Religion of Christianity. A male dominated religion that suppresses the true power of the female.

To examine the point in question, let us look at the basic concept of the men in our culture on homosexuality. Granted the intellectual tolerance of gays has raised in the past thirty years, however, what about the standard opinion of most heterosexual men in our culture? Have you ever heard these statements referring to homosexuals? "Hey, I don't understand it, but to each his own," or how about, "I have nothing against gays as long as they don't hit on me."

Men's loving of one another is not a new concept; it has been around for eons. During the Greek and the Roman Empire, homosexuality was a culturally accepted way of life. It is not spoken of in Christianity, but even Jesus dealt with his love of his twelve disciples.

What makes a man homosexual, heterosexual or even bi-sexual? Is it an urge or a choice? If it is an urge, then it is animalistic. It comes from the instinct of self preservation, the urge for sexual gratification and/or procreation. Now, we as men being capable of controlling these urges do so by choosing how and with whom we share this experience; it is both an urge and a choice. Most men in this society are raised with the religious dogma that homosexuality is wrong. The 80 percent of non-thinkers mentioned earlier never question that. Could it be that because they do not understand, and continue to follow the programming that teaches men not to love one another in a tender way, that they actually fear their own emotions?

I am not promoting or condemning homosexuality, just merely looking at a concept existing in our culture. The Wiccan religion is called a Goddess religion. For men to find their place in a Goddess religion, they first need to examine and understand their basic nature. As it says above the door of the Temple of Delphi, *"Know Thyself."*

In Wicca, the triple aspects of the Goddess are: the *Maiden, Mother and Crone*, these are revered and worshipped. Each aspect is examined, experienced and taught to the women and to the men. What about the triple aspect of the God: the *Rove, Father and Sage*? These seem to be lightly touched upon in modern Wicca or Paganism. Modern men need to examine, explore and fully experience these aspects of the God.

In this way men can better understand themselves. For a man to truly understand the Goddess, he must first understand himself. Now you might be saying, "I do understand myself." Do you really? Do we really know ourselves or are we just recognizing the experiences we have accumulated during this incarnation? Do we really know our essence? That part of us that was here before time began? There have been many names or labels slapped upon this essence; Gods, Nature, Deity, Supreme Being, the Force…. Just to mention a few. Think about this, do we even know what the term gender is, beyond its label, aside from the obvious physical differences, of course. Let's look at a theory for a moment.

Where does everything come from according to basic Paganism? Answer: *the Spirit*. The next logical question would be what is Spirit? Answer: *the life force that flows through and is everything*. That is no answer. That is just smooth words that give us no description. No one knows actually what Spirit is. Not science nor religion or even philosophy. If no one truly knows what Spirit is, then it must be the unknown or the X-factor. However, belief in this unknown spirit gives it, at least in the mental realm some sort of validity, if nothing else, validity to the believer. Logical reasoning says that the universe and everything in it had to come from something, in Wicca that something is called Spirit.

Now let's look at our world and our reason upon it. In our reality, according to the Eight Universal laws, creation occurs only through the operation of the Universal Law of Gender. As stated in the first chapter, for anything to be created, whether it is human, animal or plant life, the male plants a seed inside the female and after a period of incubation, the product is brought forth directly from the female aspect. This applies through all levels of manifestations even down to the atomic level as well as into the mental level in dealing with the conscious and subconscious mind. Both of these combined aspects are what we call Spirit; but what about Homosexuals? You might ask. Well I believe even in a Homosexual relationship, one takes on the role of the masculine aspect and the other takes on the role of the feminine aspect.

Now let's look at another path of reasoning. In the Charge of the Goddess by Doreen Valianti, it says, *"I am the beauty of the green earth and the white moon and the mysteries of the waters, from me all things proceed and unto me they must return...I have been with you from the beginning and I am that which is attained at the end of desire."* This clearly states that she is everything and everything comes from her. She is the end result of all desires, choices and decisions that we make. If this is true, everything that exists is feminine energy in different forms of manifestations, including males. Male energy is nothing more than externalized feminine energy. Granted the Charge of the Goddess is not an ancient script nor do any of us have to believe it. We are merely using it as a point of reference to examine this theory.

Charles Leland in "The Gospel of the Witches" further exemplifies this premise: *"Diana was the first created before all creation; in her were all things. Out of herself came the darkness, she divided herself; herself and her other half - Lucifer, her brother and son, was the light. And when Diana saw that the light was so beautiful, she yearned for it with exceedingly great desire. Wishing to receive the light again into her darkness, she trembled with desire. That desire was the dawn...She spun the lives of all mankind; all things were spun from the Wheel of Life from Diana. And Lucifer turned the Wheel."*

The Christian Bible even gives some credence to this theory. In Genesis it states "In the Beginning the earth (our Mother) was void and without form," (unmanifested feminine energy) "And darkness was upon the face of the deep." (The darkness was possibly referred to as Diana's darkness). The next line states,

"And the Spirit of God moved upon the face of the waters and God said, "let there be light and there was light; and the light was divided from the darkness."

Could this mean that when feminine energy begins to move, the un-manifested becomes manifested and that movement is what we classify as masculine energy?

While researching the root of the word masculine, I found it interesting that in the dictionary I was using, the word mascot was just above it. The root word of masculine is the Latin word "mas" for male. The root word for mascot is the French word "masco" which means witch. Putting two and two together, masculine energy is the mascot of the original feminine (witch) energy.

Here is another point of interest. All human babies are created in the womb as females. Only when the Y chromosome is developed later does the child express itself as male. Now I realize that this point of view may create controversy even among Pagan/Wiccan men. However, this is only one perspective out of many, after all, opinions vary. But if nothing else, it does give one something to think about while one is upon the path of self-enlightenment and truly trying to "Know Thyself."

The Goddess IS; all energy; she can never be

created or destroyed. She just IS.

The God is the perpetual transmutation of Her radiant energy; The God of Change!

This is the projective power of the male force. The ability to make change occur according to one's will.

In the next few chapters, we will examine this force through the stages of manhood as: *Rove, Father* and *Sage*. We will harvest, develop and refine this power which is inherent in every man and thus take his rightful place in the Goddess Religion.

III A Witch's Power

Before we discuss the specific power of the male witch, let's look at the latent power of Witchcraft that is in everyone. This may give us a basic understanding of ourselves and the religion of Wicca/Paganism.

The power of a Witch has been the subject of discussion among cowans (non-witches) and witches for thousands of years. There have been numerous thoughts and theories as to what exactly that power is. This power has been attributed to everything from mythological fantasy to arcane esoteric systems. All of these ideas have some basis of fact, but lack a full description of what and from where this mysterious power comes from.

The power raised and used by a witch has been labeled many things over the years. Whether you believe it is energy, psychic powers, Magick, the Will of God, the power of Satan or demonic forces, personal power, the ways of nature or any other name you may place on it, these are just labels. To name or label this force does not change its nature or its effectiveness.

Practitioners of the Craft view magic as the manipulation of forces and energies not yet understood by science, but for those who understand the scientific principles on which it is based, it is not "magical" at all.

Witches know that being able to tap into unseen worlds is essential to living the magical life, of being one with nature and your deities. When you concentrate your efforts and energy on a spell, you have shifted your consciousness. When you prepare for ritual, your brain activity slows. Your subconscious mind begins to act in accord with your conscious mind and together they are able to help you focus on your magical goal.

It is in this state that you are able to project you consciousness into other places or realms. It may appear as a dream, but these projections are very real. Just because they are not tangible does not make them unreal. After all, it is within your mind that Magick begins to take place.

Once you have focused and begun to attain your goal, how does it manifest itself? How are you able to make things happen? What attracts the successful result of your spell work or ritual? Again, we turn to a scientific explanation.

Consider raw power, such as lightening. Lightening is an electrical discharge that occurs when atmospheric conditions are set in a certain pattern, such as a storm. Science tells us that lightening will occur as a storm cloud fluctuates and the positive particles and negative particles in the cloud separate. The positively charged particles move to the upper part of the cloud and the electrons or negatively charged particles move to the bottom or lower region. Similar particles are present on the Earth's surface. The positive particles on the Earth's surface interact with the negative particles of the cloud and sets off a discharge of energy as ground to cloud lightening.

A Witch's power works in a similar process. Inside the human body, the positive and negative particles may fluctuate and create an electro-magnetic sphere around the body. Like the cloud, our positive particles move to the center or away from the outside edges. In turn, the negatively charged particles move to the extremities and edges of the body. This sets up a metaphysical discharge between the negative particles at the edge of the body and the positive particles that exist in the physical environment surrounding the body.

The question then becomes, "What causes this fluctuation in the body?" To understand, we must compare religious thought and scientific fact. A Witch raises personal power and brings it to a peak through physical and emotional activity such as sexual intercourse, chanting, dancing or running, to name a few. Gerald Gardner taught that these activities along with light binding or light scourging created and controlled blood flow throughout the body. The Christian Bible says that blood is the "life force." If blood is the life force, perhaps this is the original water that is spoken of in the bible before anything was created when it is stated "the Spirit of God moved upon the face of the waters". If one takes the words from the old gospel song, "There is power, power, power, wonderful working power in the blood," then one has to assume that the fluctuation in the charges of the body to create the electro-magnetic sphere about the body is caused by the movement of blood throughout the body.

The negative particles in the body are implanted with images of the desire through ritual in altered states of consciousness. This emotional and physical activity creates blood flow or movement. This causes the charges to move to the outer edges of the body. A polarity is set up for the negative particles to attract positive particles in physical existence, to draw or make a thing happen or occur according to the Law of Magnetism. This theory explains the physical power of the Witch, but what of the psychic powers?

The psychic power produced in Witchcraft is the power of the mind. All human beings have it. One does not have to be a witch to be psychic. Practitioners of Wicca take the time and patience to learn and cultivate this power.

For a better understanding, let's examine the conscious and subconscious mind. In actuality we only have one mind, but for the purpose of study it has been divided into various categories: conscious, subconscious, unconscious, super conscious, etc. We are going to utilize the concepts of the conscious and subconscious mind.

The conscious mind has been described as being the part of us that decides or chooses. It reasons inductively and deductively. Deductive reasoning means that the conscious mind takes an assimilation of facts and reasons down to the logical conclusion. This can be compared to a prosecuting attorney who presents facts or evidence to prove the defendant is guilty of a crime. The conscious mind is the "thinker" inside of us. The only power it has is the power of choice.

The subconscious mind is the "doer" or activator. It reasons only inductively. Inductive reasoning means it starts with the conclusion or answers first and tries to fit the facts or evidence to that result. Like the defense attorney in comparison. He/she starts with the conclusion "not guilty" and matches the evidence to fit. The subconscious mind believes and diligently works to produce the effects of the end result. This is according to psychology and the studies done on the mind of man mainly in the past 100 years.

In Witchcraft, the conscious and subconscious are recognized as the Lord and Lady or the God and Goddess. The conscious mind is masculine, linear, analytical and "the GOD" within; the subconscious mind is feminine, intuitive and manifested as "the GODDESS" within.

When the magician is in an altered state of consciousness as in ritual, a sort of self hypnosis takes place and the spiritual act of creation occurs. Whether in the physical or spiritual realms the act of creation is the same, that is: the male plants the seed (in this concept, the seed is the idea) inside the female and after a period of incubation, the seed is always produced directly by the female part.

With this analogy one can easily see how magic or psychic powers are developed. It must also be noted that this phenomenon occurs positively or negatively according to the thoughts, intentions and belief system of the individual's mind. Therefore it would be advisable to guard one's thought world well.

Another aspect to a Witch's power is communion. A Witch attunes themselves to the cycles and seasons of the Earth and her elements. The power of the changing seasons of life, death and rebirth, are the basis of Witchcraft and why witches refer to the earth as our Mother.

Although many Witches live in the city, many prefer to live in the country to be better able to commune with these energies. This is not to say that Pagans living in the city cannot achieve this same communion. Many powerful and spiritual Witches live in highly populated metropolitan areas. They have managed to find ways to honor the Goddess, the earth and the energy within. This takes a bit more effort if you walk out your door into downtown traffic instead of an open field of lush greenery, but it is no problem for a witch.

Whether in the city or the country, planting gardens, growing herbs and working with nature is an essential part of the Craft. The cycles of the earth are as intrinsic to our growth as the budding of a plant or the coming of winter. The system is subtle, yet powerful. Putting yourself in harmony with these energies awakens the ability to feel the energy of life flow through you.

This is the power of a Witch. And yes, it does express itself differently in men than it does in women. So, let's examine how this power flows through the male Witch.

IV. The Masculine and Feminine Force

For thousands of years the so-called battle of the sexes has raged on between men and women. This is the battle of man's power against woman's power, mainly because men and women do not understand why the male and female, aside from the physical differences, are so opposite in their internal make-up. For eons, men in general have considered the woman as the weaker sex. This is due to the erroneous comparison of men's superior physical strength.

In nature it is primarily the males of the species who do most of the fighting for dominance over the females. This is due to the procreation urge to continually propagate the species. Early man noticed that in nature the seed was numerous compared to the fertile womb. An oak tree, for example, will drop thousands of acorns upon the ground and only very few oak trees will develop or take root and grow. In human beings, a man has over 200,000 spermatozoa ejaculating into a womb with a single egg. However, only one will fertilize the egg. All of the others will fall by the wayside.

This law applies to the animal kingdom as well, with a ratio of one male to multiple females, for example, in deer, one buck can service seven to twelve does or in chickens one rooster can service ten hens. This is true of most gregarious or herd type animals including humans. The seed is more plentiful than the fertile womb.

Now let us look at the physical characteristics of the phenomena. The males in nature are usually more flamboyant in their appearance, such as the male peacock has all the beautiful feathers, whereas the female is rather brown and drab. The male lion has a huge mane while the female does not. In nature this is true of most animal species. Even in humans the man is generally more hairy and they have beards.

The idea here is that in nature, only the strongest survive. Animals do not think individually, they think with a group mind for the perpetuation of the species, through their physical expression and spirit. Yes, they do express emotions such as anger, greed, and loyalty; however, they do not express self-pity because their perceptions are guided by instinct which is group oriented within the Spirit. An example of this concept, as it applies to nature can be seen on the television series Star Trek and their characters "The Borg". There is no "I am I" awareness in nature. All is connected and interactive.

This underlying issue of instinct is apparently

innate in human beings; however because of our gift of reasoning, the intellect has soared to the forefront of human evolution. The ability to reason and think inwardly and individually is what has put us at the top of the food chain. This ability is both a gift and a curse in itself. On the one hand, we can perceive the higher meaning of life through our rationalization beyond the physical realm. This does however mean in order to accomplish this we have necessarily separated ourselves from the main source in order to recognize it. It's like the old expression, "You can't see the forest for the trees"; unless you see it from a distance, but then you are not a part of it any longer.

From this perspective, one can understand why there has been a void in the standard of relationships between modern man and woman. Most men do not understand a woman's physical, mental and emotional make up. And most women do not understand why men act, think and react the way they do. It has to do with the perpetual transmutation of radiant energy at the essence of their being. Simply put, men are basically projective and women are basically receptive by nature. This not only applies to the physical expression, but in the mental, emotional and spiritual realms as well. Men and women think and react differently to the same physical, mental and emotional stimuli or situation.

Years ago, I watched a documentary on the differences between men and women. They were testing the response by males and females to the same exact problem solving situations. In one test that was conducted on eighteen-month-old babies, ten boys and ten girls, they sat them in a chair in front of a television screen with pleasant scenes to their senses appearing every eight seconds. All of the babies loved this. Then they suspended a rope down just in front of them while they were watching the screen. At random times, the television screen was abruptly shut off. All of the children were somewhat upset and all of them began to play with the rope. When they pulled on the rope the television would come back on for a few minutes and then would shut off again. The children soon learned to pull the rope to get the television playing again. The test was to see if there would be a different reaction between the boys and the girls if they pulled on the rope and the television didn't come back on.

It was amazing. All ten of the boys would pull once and if the television didn't come back on, they would pull harder and jerk the rope several times as if to force the television to come on again. All ten of the girls did the same thing up to a point. They pulled the rope once, then twice but then if the television didn't come back on; they would all start crying.

Another test they did was to take ten men and ten women that were all the same age and background. They put each one in a MRI machine to trace the blood flow in the brain. The men and women were given simple problem solving equations for them to come to logical answers. All of the men and women came up with the exact same answers. The results were that when the men were concentrating and utilizing their brain activity, the blood in their brain was rushing to the outer edges of their brain. The blood in the women's brains rushed to the center of their brains. The conclusion of the test was that even though men and women rationalize the same; but they us different pathways of the brain to come to the same conclusion. Therefore, men and women think differently. The basic difference in men and women then would be that women's perception of life comes to them from the right hemisphere of the brain. This is the intuitive, imaginative, emotional and receptive part of the brain. Men, however, perceive life through the left hemisphere of the brain, which is the analytical, mathematical, linear and projective part of the brain.

This may in fact be mainly due to the physical side of our expression. As far as energy flow through the human body, male and female are the same energy yet opposites, projective and receptive polarity in nature.

Let's see if we can define a simplistic example of male and female sexuality. To understand how men and women are opposite ends of the same creative energy, imagine if you will a male and female standing, facing one another with only an inch between them. This one-inch space is filled with the Supreme Spirit flowing from the Etheric realm. Now imagine two cones about twelve inches long and the wide-open ends attached to each other with both points of the cones facing opposite directions.

Now place these cones as if superimposing them upon the male and female standing close to one another. Place the cones at the genital area. Make the cone over the female red in color. Now if the Spirit wishes to express a projective body then the male image will turn red to match the cone. If however, the Spirit wishes to express a receptive body, then the female would turn red to match the cone. The cone itself does not change only whether it is externalized in the male or internalized in the female. One is projective and the other is receptive.

In old myths and legends, this projective power of the male has been depicted as the God of Transmutation, the Lord of Death and Resurrection, the

God of CHANGE! The ability to take whatever energy exists and transmutes it into another form.

The feminine power of receptiveness has been depicted as the power to create and birth it into existence. The power of creation! But according to the scientific law of "perpetual transmutation of radiant energy", energy, ALL energy, is never created or destroyed, it just is, and change is its only attribute. Could it be that what we call creation and destruction are merely illusionary labels so our finite minds can discern and measure this transmutation or change of everlasting, omnipotent energy?

If that is true then maybe this Goddess energy, this feminine force which is inside all of us is that part of us that comprehends the Higher Knowledge and the ultimate meaning of life far beyond the known facts of science and physics and in an abstract way, keeps us connected to the Spiritual aspect of life itself.

Females, because of their physical make-up, might be more directly connected to this Goddess energy than males are, wouldn't you think?

However, the male, because of his physical make-up is more directly connected with the God force which is the ability to take a seed, idea, a concept directly from the astral realm and project it into this physical reality. By the old magical axiom, *"making change occur in accordance with one's will."*

V The Basic Nature of Men

For most modern men who are starting upon their spiritual path in Paganism today, they are first confronted with the need to understand their basic nature. Cultural concepts say that "man" is an intellectual and emotional being. Men do have these attributes but the basic nature of men is animalistic and instinctual. And these attributes are what modern men have lost touch with.

These urges and instincts still operate within us, because we are animals that have evolved into humans. Over the course of history, this idea has been overlooked, forgotten, or at the least tried to be ignored by humanity.

This has partially been due to the development of civilization and the growth of the individual ego. The idea that man was a distinct and separate creation from the rest of living creation was developed through the "I AM I" awareness of self-consciousness in humans about the time that religion came into being.

As stated earlier the animal thought process is oriented to group mind. They do not think inwardly like human beings. A horse in the pasture withstanding the cold sleet and rain feels the pain and discomfort and accepts it. The horse does not think to himself, "How cruel it is of my master to leave me out here unprotected and without shelter," as a human would.

The animal is led and guided through its life by urges and instincts which it has no choice but to act on. Here the main distinction between animals and humans is, though man has the same urges and instincts, he also has the gift of reasoning. Man has the ability to choose whether or not to act on the instincts and urges he feels. The five primary urges and instincts are inherent in humans and as men, part of our basic nature. These urges are unconsciously effecting and influencing our physical, emotional and intellectual systems of our lives. They are directly connected to the five functional systems of the body (sight, hearing, smell, touch and taste), which in turn influences our emotional system. This also effects our attitudes and thought processes.

The five primary urges and instincts that are at the core of essence in human beings are as follows:

1. Self preservation – The self preservation urge is the core or root of the other primary urges or instincts. All of the other urges are derived from self preservation. This instinct is the one that keeps us alive. Primitive man especially needed it to survive the wildness of nature. It lets us know when there is danger or physical threat to our existence. The self preservation instinct also communicates to us by a "knowing" or confidence in what is needed or beneficial to our survival. Without this urge we would simply cease to exist because we would not feel the need to fight or struggle to live. We would simply give up.

2. Self-expression - This urge allows us to express ourselves, our nature. Every animal or human, everything is an expression of the Spirit, but each one is unique and individualized. Some expressions in this urge are limited by form. For example: A rose cannot express itself as a dandelion. In man this urge sometimes is suppressed by the cultural environment the person has grown up in. The self expression urge allows us to express our emotions, both the negative and positive emotions alike. This is accomplished through our personalities and there are four personality temperaments, which are sanguine, choleric, melancholy and phlegmatic. These personality temperaments are fully covered in Florence Litenhauer's book, "The Personality Tree."

3. The Creative Urge - This urge is also known as the sex drive. Initially in the animalistic term, this urge was for procreation. The instinct is the need to create or to re-create an expression of Spirit in another life form. The urge in humans has developed into a desire for sexual intercourse mainly for pleasure. In our culture, men especially have been taught since childhood that sex is for self-gratification primarily and that having children is a secondary consideration. There is nothing wrong with this concept except that it doesn't address the basic function of the instinct or urge. When men feel the testosterone levels in the system surge, they naturally take it to the sexual outlet for expression, not understanding they, "by choice", could sublimate the urge into a mental, emotional or spiritual level of expression. Our history is full of great men and women who utilized this energy to become artists, musicians, writers or successful business leaders by sublimating the energy of the creative urge or instinct.

4. Will to Power - This urge is a direct link to action. The ability to fortify determination through action. The energy of the Will to Power urge brings up the spirit of competition. To insure the perpetuation of the species, the males would fight for the right to be alpha male so that the strongest of the gene pool would be passed onto the next generation. This urge now operates through the ego instead of the higher self. More for self attained glory rather than the betterment of the all. In other words, "The needs of the one outweigh the needs of the many."

5. Gregarious or Herd Urge - When the herd urge changes its rhythm, our desire to be around people or to be alone manifests. Humans are gregarious by nature. We have always gathered together in tribes, clans, villages, towns or cities. In the animal aspect, it is for growth, safety and power. There is strength in numbers. There are times, though, when the urge is low and then we feel the desire to be alone. Primarily to relax or for rest and recuperation, to regenerate, so to speak.

Here is an example: When fear strikes us the heart starts pumping faster so the circulatory system can get more blood to the extremities of the body such as the feet and arms. Adrenaline pumps through the body to burn up excess calories and the mind abandons rational thought. The entire system is gearing up for the fight or flight syndrome. Primitive man needed this syndrome for survival. Now think about this, worry is an emotion stemming from fear, which has already been stated is from the self-preservation urge or instinct. When we worry over something, like not having the money to pay the electric bill, the same physical, emotional and mental process takes place inside us, only we don't have to express the fight or flight syndrome.

Therefore, the emotional and nervous, emotional and circulatory systems of the body get backed up and clogged. As a result, negative nervous, emotional and mental conditions are developed.

A correlation of how instincts unconsciously affect our modern life as men is the Will to Power urge. In nature this urge is expressed to insure the most healthy and strongest genes are passed on through the herds to insure the continuation of the species. In young men this urge is expressed when they feel the need to fight, battle or struggle for dominance, which is controlled now by the ego for self gain instead of prosperity of all as it is in the animal kingdom.

Another aspect of the urges and instincts are that they can be in balance or out of balance either to the high or low side. A person with the self preservation urge out of balance to the high side would express this in their life as being greedy, miserly or become a hoarder, constantly stocking more than they could consume or need. The urge on the high side would stimulate the fear of lack or the feeling of the supply not meeting the demand and that emotion would institute the action in the individual as greediness and selfishness.

If the self-preservation urge were on the low side, the person might be shiftless and lazy to the point of not meeting their immediate needs at all. They would not look forward and prepare for the near future and would live from week to week or from hand to mouth, so to speak.

A person with the self-preservation urge in balance would, in their mundane life, take measures to secure their immediate needs and put a little something away for a rainy day.

These urges and instincts are inherent in both men and women, but in men they are externalized, whereas in women they are internalized in their expression.

The best symbolic explanation of this is by comparing the feminine force to all the bodies of water on the earth, such as the oceans, seas and lakes, etc. The masculine force would be in movement, such as the rivers, streams and tributaries that flow out of and into the bodies of water.

Men, therefore express the five primary urges and instincts in their essence from the inside out. Almost as if they put everything they are or what they think they are on the outside for the whole world to see.

Now, don't misunderstand my definitions. I am not stereotyping all men and women into one standard. I am talking about the essence of humans not their personalities. That would take up another book. However, a point to keep in mind here is that the urges and instincts do affect our personalities at the unconscious level.

It is easy to understand the basic nature of men if we understand our basic urges and instincts. In so doing, we not only comprehend intellectually who or what we are but also why we act the way we do. Running away from or ignoring our basic nature only creates stress and bewilderment in our true essence of the human expression of the Spirit.

Now, let us examine the stages of manhood and correlate these urges and instincts with how they operate through the *Rove, the Father and the Sage* stages of manhood.

VI The Rove Stage of Man

In Wicca as a religion there are two natural cycles that are studied and related to; as they have an effect over our physical, mental, emotional and spiritual lives. These are the lunar and solar cycles.

The moon cycles are considered to be our intuitive and subjective aspects of our internal make up so to speak and generally associated as being feminine energy. The reason for this according to ancient thought and scientific fact is that the moon has a cycle of twenty eight days; the equivalent to a woman's menstrual cycle.

The moon represents the Goddess through its phases of the new moon, full moon and dark moon as the Maiden, the Mother and the Crone or the Hag.

The solar cycle follows the birth, life, death and rebirth of the God. It is called the wheel of the year and is by most Pagans associated as masculine energy.

Men and women have both energies within themselves, God and Goddess respectively. It is merely at the physical level that one or the other expresses more dominantly. Depending on that expression, shows whether the person is tuned into either the lunar or solar cycle.

Since we are discussing men, we will concentrate our attention on the solar cycle, however, it must be remembered that this does not mean that women are excluded from this cycle for it represents a major part of their life as well.

The solar cycle represents the entire life of humans from birth to death, shortened down to a time span of twelve months. The average life span is approximately seventy years long. The wheel of the year marks the eight major rites of passages that the God encounters throughout his life. It also represents the rites of passages that we encounter in our lives. These are called the Sabbats and they mark the seasonal agricultural times of the year.

Yule is the rebirth of the God, the child of promise, the promise of bringing warmth back to the earth in the springtime. The Goddess is in her Maiden/Mother aspect. Yule is celebrated at the Winter Solstice, December 21st. This is the shortest day of the year and the longest night.

Imbolg is the next Sabbat and it is celebrated on February 1st. It symbolizes the God at puberty. The Goddess is seen in her nurturing aspect. Imbolg is a festival of lights as it is a time of illumination for the God. Puberty means he is going through the internal as well as external changes. He is beginning to learn about his sexuality. A whole new world has opened up to him.

Spring Equinox, the next Sabbat, falls on March 21st. This is the Sabbat that begins to coincide with the inseminator stage of manhood. Springtime is a time for planting seeds, a time for fertility. This Sabbat celebrates new beginnings, a time when the deadness of winter is cast off and nature springs to live again.

In looking at the triple aspect of the God as we do the Goddess, we begin here at the Rove stage. The time that men reach this stage varies with each man. It may well begin in some men as early as thirteen years of age and in some go well beyond the age of thirty-five, generally though it is between the ages of sixteen and twenty-five.

The Rove stage is that time in a man's life when he feels the thrill of the hunt, whether it be hunting animals or women, or in our modern society, the hunting of our employment, this feeling is an urge or instinct and very animalistic by nature. It is called the creative urge or sex drive. Humans, after all, are still animals regardless how civilized we have become. Most men in our culture have been taught that it is wrong to have, or especially give in to these urges. As stated in the previous chapters, the reason for this is that human beings evolved to a point in our history that our consciousness began to believe that we were divinely created and our animal heritage became an embarrassment. So we try not to acknowledge our inherited urges and instincts from our animal ancestors. These urges must be controlled in our modern civilization, but to ignore them can be very detrimental to ones understanding of their own basic nature.

The Rove stage of men and the God has three sub-aspects that are also worth studying. These can be found in the diagram of the triple aspect of the God at the end of this chapter. These sub-aspects are the hunter, the lover and the protector.

The hunter sub-aspect of the Rove is the young man's passion for the chase. The young Rove derives pleasure from this primarily due to the self preservation urge or instinct. Ultimately, deep below the conscious level, it matters little whether the Rove is actually the hunter or the prey. It is basically the sensation of anticipation and the adrenalin that flows when trying to control the outcome of the chase. In just about every action movie there is a big chase scene, because the audience thrills over this sensation and it holds you on the edge of your seat, as they say.

The lover sub-aspect deals directly with the creative urge. The old expression used by old men when they see a courting young man was, "He sure was full of piss and vinegar." This expression means the young man was crazy with lust. When the testosterone starts pumping in a man, especially a young man in his Rove aspect, he is literally invoking Cernunnos or Pan within himself. These two God forms have been called the wildness inside of us. Through the creative urge this wildness flows and demands to be expressed. Thank goodness humans can control this through their will to power urge or life as we know it would be a continuous Bacchanalia.

   The young Rove today should be free spirited in this aspect. He should be free to choose and have as many willing partners as he wants, with the understanding by both parties that there are no strings attached. He should fully explore this aspect of his manhood, utilizing safe sexual practices, of course, to fully understand his nature. By the same token, women in their maiden aspect of life should adopt the same attitudes.

   What about love you may ask? Love is an emotion and like all other emotions you have the choice as to whether you wish to feel them or not. For example: Nobody can make you feel mad or angry by their actions or words. It is only an invitation for you to express and feel that emotion. The choice is yours whether to take the invitation or decline it. It is the same with love.

We are speaking here of romantic love, not universal love. Universal love is the genuine feeling of, Oneness that connects all of us together and not just people, but all of us, the plants, the animals, Gods and the cosmos. Romantic love is an illusion that two or more people agree to create by their commitments to one another. Often times, people in relationships, not understanding this create the illusion without the consent or agreement of the other individual and ultimately with the relationship. In creating this illusion one major point to consider are the ideas that have been with man since he first became aware of his emotions.

The ways of the Mother are powerful. When one fully understands the forces with which we work and to a degree controls those forces - it is an awesome responsibility. "To thine own self be true," means honor. Honor is a gift one gives to themselves. It is your integrity. When you learn the higher understandings of the forces that exist, you can control them. When you ignore them or do not put the knowledge of them into ethical practice in your life, is to dishonor yourself and the Gods. This is very dangerous!

Sex is sacred to the Mother. It is a sacred act or

ritual and it's a creative act of magic. If a witch (male or female), copulates with another for pure pleasure, especially if their partner doesn't understand the full responsibility of the act, then that witch is dishonoring themselves and harming their partner in the higher planes. When the two forces are united in the act of sexual intercourse there is a collision of energies that form a vortex that expands all the way up through the seven component levels of human beings. Remember, "All acts of love and pleasure are Her rituals." There is no casual sex for the sake of sex; it always includes mental, emotional, and spiritual energies mixing together.

This is what Sir Lancelot meant when he spoke to Queen Guinevere in "The Mists of Avalon" by Marion Zimmer Bradley; in the heat of passion he stopped and said, "My Lady, I cannot and will not dishonor you in this way!" This was because she didn't understand the responsibility in the higher planes of their union.

It is also normal for the man in his Rove stage to express the sub-aspect called the Protector. The Protector sub-aspect of the Rove stage in manhood comes from Paleolithic times. It was recognized early on that men had upper body strength. When the female was giving birth or nurturing the young through her maternal instincts she was vulnerable to harm. Since survival was prevalent during this time period, the male, unencumbered with the young took the role as protector, a guardian of the clan. The younger and stronger males adapted to this role quite naturally and eventually became known in many cultures as the warriors. This concept is still promoted today in the form of super heroes who fight injustice and help those in need.

Boys and men are attracted to these stories because they tap into the protector aspect of us and speak directly to our manhood. This is how the Rove aspect of the God of Witchcraft, in all of his sub-aspects operates and flows through all men. All we have to do is recognize Him, call to Him and commune with Him. This can be done through meditations, rituals and rites of passages.

Magical Tools of the Rove

The standard magical tools of modern Wicca are the four elemental tools: *the pentacle, the wand, the athame and the cauldron*. The explanation of these tools can be found in many books about Wicca on the market today. They are mentioned here to correlate the four elemental tools of the Rove which are *the shield*, *the spear, the sword and the bow*. There are three sets of tools that can be utilized in men's mysteries, a set for each stage of manhood. These tools or weapons are not an absolute necessity for everyone; however, they do enhance the trance or altered state of consciousness in ritual. The tools can be charged and consecrated in a ceremony and infused with power by the magician.

Each tool represents an element. By working with these tools, the Rove gains elemental power. Gaining elemental power is to work with that element to understand it and to recognize it within oneself. Once you learn to control that, which is internal, within your being, you can control it outwardly as well. This is the basis of all Magick; simply stated, "As it is above, so shall it be below."

Here is an explanation of the four tools of the Rove state and their associations:

The Shield: Many shields are made of various materials such as wood, metal or leather. The shape is up to the owner and creator. The main thing is to make it personal decorate it, cleanse it, charge it and USE IT!

The shield represents the direction of North, the element of earth. It is the foundation of your manhood. It contains everything that you are. It is what you have brought with you into this incarnation and what you have done with it so far in your life. It is your goals and aspirations of what you want to achieve with the rest of your life. Its associations and uses are for strength, stability, protection, guardians, fertility, grounding energies and the transformation of gateways into other realms.

The Spear: The spear can be made with a metal head or a sharp pointed wooden instrument, such as a javelin. The spear represents the direction of east and the element of air. The spear as a weapon is utilized in many varied motions. It is thrust like a sword, thrown towards a target or whirled around like a staff. The spear has the ability to be many weapons in one, depending on the situation. It is seen as having many perspectives or perceptions; therefore, the spear is associated with the intellect or reasoning. Like intelligence it is not narrow minded, seeing only one perspective. Its associations are the winds, winged creatures, linear thinking, sunrise, new beginnings and mind energy.

The Sword: The sword is usually double edged like a broad sword, but not necessarily. The sword is the warrior's ability to slash through inertia. It is the action behind thought. The sword symbolizes determination, excitement and enthusiasm. Its direction is south, the element of fire. The sword is the Rove's symbol of authority, the power to instigate Magick. Like Excalibur, the sword makes the warrior king of his own choices and responsible to them. Its associations are heat, flames, passion, movement, endurance, goal accomplishment and lightening bolts.

The Bow: The archer, with his bow and arrow, is the epitome of focusing the power of the will upon a chosen thought. The bow is the power in a Rove to utilize faculties within him to never give up, regardless what the odds are. The bow is confidence or faith, with no acceptance of any other outcome save the desired goal. Its direction is west, the element of water. Its associations are strong emotions, sunset, completion, storms, rain and bodies of water.

It must be stated that these tools represent the internal mechanisms of the psychology of the Rove stage of manhood. They are to be used magically; but also practiced physically. This can be done with the use of kata's. The kata is a form of meditation with the weapon in movement, a somewhat of a slow dance motion utilized in the martial arts. Learning some kata's with each tool and using them in a meditation or a ritual setting, helps to gain the elemental power of each tool. Any simple kata from any of the forms of martial arts will do, just keep it personal with the intent of the form for internal growth in mind when deciding which is best for you.

The Rove stage of manhood is *beginning to recognize and develop the masculine energies of the male, which will in time be refined and cultivated into the Father and Sage stages of manhood.* If you are at the Rove stage, enjoy this time of life filled with the special magic of wonder and change of the Rove. For those who have past this stage it is never gone for good. The Father and the Sage can still call upon the Rove inside them, it never dies, and it is always there. Call upon it when there is a need for swift change or a new outlook in situations that arise in your life. For the Rove lays waiting inside every man, waiting to be expressed.

VII The Father Stage of Manhood

The Father stage of manhood coincides with the Sabbat of Beltaine. It is a time of union between the God and the Great Mother. His duty now is to promote growth; the growth of plants, hence his image of the Green Man and the growth of animals and his image of the antlered God. He has now taken the role of a man with responsibilities in assisting the continuous cycle of the Goddess. He has become the Father to all, so to speak. He will stay in this role from Beltaine through Summer Solstice, which is the peak of His power; then until the Autumn Equinox where His role will change once again.

The same energy of the Rove is now refined and focused in the Father stage. It is not as chaotic or wild as the younger Rove expression. The Father has had time to experience channeling that energy into different areas. Whereas the Rove energy was used to conquer, the Father energy takes the conquest and begins to organize it to best serve everyone.

When I was seventeen and working with my father, I always wanted to stay out late and have fun. Being full of the Rove spirit at that age I wanted to do and be everything. My father, knowing this, did not deter me from my desires. However, when it was 6:00 AM and time to get out of bed and go to work, he did teach me how to be responsible for my actions. His infamous statement to me when I had gotten to bed at 5:00 am, knowing that I had to get up at 6:00 AM was, "Son, it is okay to stay out all night with the owls, but you still have to get up with the robins in the morning."

This is the role of the Father, not so much biologically seeding children, as it is to take a more general responsible outlook to the earth, magic and life itself. One doesn't have to have children or a significant other to be in the Father stage of manhood. The call of the father is subtle and sometimes confusing to men. Chemical and psychological changes take place within the male; a process which in most cases takes years to complete. A man well into his rove stage generally is too busy to take notice of these changes in himself. He may at times be aware of certain emotions and feelings he is experiencing, however not understanding them, he may express periods of melancholy Mood swings.

Up until now he has been utilizing his rove energy in facing life situations. He becomes frustrated when his actions and attitudes no longer seem to assimilate with his life's path.

A few years ago I counseled a young man in our

church that was going through the transitional period of the Father stage. He came by the church one night and I could tell he was distraught about something. This man was thirty years old and had a good paying job. He was not married and at the time was not involved in a relationship with anyone. Jim had been a member of the church, in good standing, for two years. His mundane and spiritual life was pretty well organized and orderly. After we chit chatted for awhile there came a lull in the conversation, he furrowed his brow and said, "Terry, I'd like to talk to you about something that is going on in my life that I do not understand."

I said, "Sure, Jim, what's going on?"

He shook his head with puzzlement and said, "I don't know actually. I have been feeling weird lately. It's like I am missing something or want more out of my life. And it's not a woman or a relationship, it goes beyond that." "Jim, tell me exactly what you are feeling as best as you can?" I questioned. "Well, I feel like I need to leave my mark, so to speak, in the world. I don't want to eventually die and my life only had meaning to me. You know what I mean? And I don't understand why I'm having these feelings; because my life seems to be going fairly well. I can't figure out why this is bothering me so much. Do you have any idea what is going on with me?" I sat there a moment and then told him I felt that he was more than likely hearing the call of the Father.

The look of surprise that came over his face was like I had just slapped him. He said, "Whoa, Terry, I have no children and right now I don't want any, so how can I be hearing the call of the Father?" I then explained to him that the energy of the Father aspect does not necessarily mean that you have to seed children. That is one part of the Father; however the Father aspect of Manhood encompasses a much larger scope.

The vibration energy of the Father aspect extends not only to the physical, but into the emotional and Spiritual as well. It is the urge inside a man not only to procreate, but to expand himself out beyond his ego and into his community, thereby fulfilling the innate desire to enhance the meaning of life itself.

The Father Energy is exemplified in the story of a pair of father and son bulls standing on a hill over looking a valley full of cows. The son turns to the father bull and says, "Hey, Dad, why don't we run down there and have our way with a couple of those cows?" the father bull replies, "Tell you what son, let's walk down there and have our way with all of them."

Three months after we talked, Jim received his Fatherhood Rite of Passage. The change that took place within him was amazing. He became more focused and calmer and is now a Third Degree Priest happily accepting his responsibilities to his Gods and his community. This year he is going to be married to a woman who shares his life's goals.

The three sub-aspects of the Father begin with the *Provider*. The *Provider* urge in men is the hunter of the Rove stage. The Father still feels the thrill of the chase, but his focus is more on sustaining life not only for himself but for others as well. His scope has broadened beyond his own desires. If he is not working for his family then he is working for the whole tribe, society or culture. This stems from the gregarious or herd urge or instinct. In men, as this becomes more prominent, he begins to think of the whole instead of the one. Our primitive instincts unconsciously tell us that there is strength in numbers. An example of this in our culture would be the rookie police officer and the seasoned veteran officer. The rookie has power but hasn't learned how to be a team player as the veteran officer has. The rookie sees the glory of the job while the veteran sees the job as to serve and protect.

The *Consort* is the second sub-aspect of the Father stage. The *Consort* aspect of the God assists the Goddess in her manifestations. An allegoric perspective would be; the God is the gardener of the garden of the Goddess. He tills the soil and gets it ready for planting. He then plants the seed. The God tends the garden while the plants grow, weeding, watering and etc. until it is time to harvest the crops. Without the God the garden would still exist but it would be wild and unkempt. The job of the *Consort* is to manage the garden to bring about a specific desired end result.

In this stage, some men feel the urge to settle down and raise a family. They devote their life to providing for their family unit. However, this is only one expression of the Father. It is the one promoted by the majority of our culture, but there are other expressions as well.

Some men without family units extend this expression beyond themselves to the systems of society. In business it is the corporate executive or the chairman of the board. In politics this urge is initially expressed as serving the people. In religion, it is in the aspect of clergy. In all of these examples it is the unconscious urge of the Father aspect that guides the man in his endeavors. Now the ego may put different labels upon these desires, such as money, power and control, but the urge or instinct is the driving force.

The third sub-aspect of the Father stage is the *Magician*. In the tarot, the magician card usually means the power and knowledge to control your life. Magick by definition means the ability to understand the laws of life and the cosmos, then using that knowledge to apply, direct and manipulate those energies to a specific result.

At this stage the *Magician* inside the man learns through experience and application the rules of how his world operates. Not necessarily why, but how. This is a power of men, their linear, mathematical thinking. They see how something works; the laws involved then direct the result to a beneficial outcome. For example; if a man has a family and is providing for them, he learns the rules and customs of the culture or society in which he lives and utilizes that system to benefit his family for the best mode of living according to that culture. If the man is clergy, he studies the spiritual laws of his religion and utilizes them for the benefit of all. In the old religion these men are called shamans, medicine men and priests.

The *Magician* aspect of the Father stage stems from the will to power urge or instinct; that part of a man that drives him to perform and gather accomplishments. This is the unconscious desire to build and assist the Mother in all of her manifestations. As stated earlier, the Goddess is the wheel of life and the God turns the wheel.

Here is an explanation of the four tools of the Father state and their associations:

The Hammer: The hammer represents the direction of north and the element of earth. The hammer also represents the Father's ability to mold and shape his own destiny, like the hammer of the Celtic blacksmith God, Goibinie. It is the power to change something into something different. Its associations are midnight, construction, building, manifestation of desires and lightening bolts.

The Three-tined Pitchfork: The three-tined pitchfork stands for the direction of east and the element of air. The pitchfork represents decision, the ability to see clearly and choose. It is also a tool of transition since its three tines represent the Rove, the Father and the Sage. The Father is a stage of transition from warrior to sage much like the three nights of full moon is the peak of power of the transitions from the new to dark moon, or the transition between the waxing and waning of the moon cycle. The pitchfork associations are noon day, the sun, windstorms, planning, diagrams, maps, new ideas and all of the ace cards in the tarot.

The Double edged Axe: The double edged axe's direction is south, the element of fire. It represents the Father's ability to deliver specific action to a specific end. The ax has to be aimed for a deliberate blow. Like a laser beam, it is focused fire to a finite point of execution. The ax is the Father's power to direct his action accurately. There is no wasted energy with the ax. Its associations are targets, training of any kind, any paperwork with pen or pencil and all things that focus the mind.

The Cauldron: The cauldron represents the direction of west and the element of water. It symbolizes the Father's willingness and duty to sustain and nourish life. As the provider, the Father develops a deep emotional attachment within himself to helping the younger men on their path. The cauldron is the tool to help the Father utilize the will. Its associations are gray colors, dusk, dark waters, emotions, intuition, divinations and the specific color of blue.

VIII The Sage Stage of Manhood

In the mist of the forest, a figure stands in a dark cloak of earthen colors. His long gray hair and lengthy beard cannot hide the wrinkles upon his face placed there by time. In his hand is a gnarled staff, grasped by boney fingers. Dark and mysterious is the old man. yet there is a twinkle of mischief in his eyes, as if he knows a secret you do not.

He lifts his hand in a gesturing motion of welcome and speaks with an eerie soft voice, "So you have finally arrived. Now, do you have the courage to enter my realm?"

This is the image most people have when they hear the word Sage; the wise old wizard, who lives by himself on top of a mountain or alone in the woods.

In the wheel of the year, the Sage stage of manhood correlates with the Sabbats of Autumn Equinox and Samhain. Following the cycles of the God at Autumn Equinox, September 21st is the second harvest, and he enters eldership. His goal once again shifts and changes to focus on harvesting the seeds that have been sown which now have come to fruition.

To men, Sagehood represents utilizing one's life experiences and wisdom for the betterment of the whole. This is not to say that every old man is a Sage or that every Sage is necessarily old. In the Old Religion, the Sage has committed his life to working for the people and the growth of spirituality more so than his own egocentric self. In modern paganism the Sage is looked upon as one who has lived a pagan lifestyle long enough to have valuable information and experience in the Mysteries spoken about in most books on the Craft.

Within my community there are about 600 Pagans, Wiccans, and Druids, in the Tri-Sate area that I associate with. In this area I am accepted as a Sage. There are a lot of young people that I counsel with that refer to me as "The Old Man". This is not an insult; it is rather a title of respect. Because when I talk to them, they listen. They actually want to hear my opinion. Do they always take my advice? Heavens no! But at least they are interested in what I have to say.

There are about twenty children in our church congregation ranging in ages from two years old to ten years old. They all call me Pa Pa. One day some people were fishing in the small country pond down the road from the church. As they drove by, they stopped to talk to me about our pet goats. It was on a Saturday, so seven or eight children were visiting the church with their parents, as they often do. The people and I were standing by the goat pen talking, and all the children were running and playing all around us. After awhile one of the ladies asked, "Are all of these kids your grandchildren, they are all calling you Pa Pa?" I said, "No, not by blood, but to a lot of them I am the only Pa Pa they got, and I love them as if they were my own grandchildren." The lady, who wasn't pagan, replied, "Well, that's a great outlook for a church minister to have."

Sagehood calls to men when they feel a family type love towards people whether they be Kith or Kin or not. Let us look at the three sub-aspects of the Sage to get a better understanding of this stage of manhood.

The first sub-aspect is the *Counselor*. The *Counselor* aspect of Sagehood follows the protector stage of the Rove and the provider stage of the Father. The Sage, having gained many years experience as the Protector and Provider now spends much of his time teaching and advising the young Roves and Fathers upon their life's path.

One of the problems with our culture today is the growing indifference to the elderly. The idea among a lot of the people is that if one is old their knowledge and wisdom is outdated and of very little use in today's fast paced computerized world. Old people seem to be in the way and troublesome. Our society tends to ignore them because we just don't have the time, with our rush-a-day lifestyles. I am reminded of the words in a country song, "I'm in a hurry to get things done, I rush and rush till life's no fun, all I really have to do is live and die, and I'm in a hurry and don't know why." At Sagehood, this is the way a man begins to look at life, he finally realizes that there is no need to hurry through life and starts to take life a little easier.

The second sub-aspect of the Sage is the *Wise man* or *Grandfather* aspect. This is the aspect of the Sage that everyone loves, the kindly old gentleman who is sincerely concerned about everyone else. He intently listens to what others have to say, reads between the words and knows the emotion behind them. People trust the grandfather. He knows what life lessons are ahead for others because he has lived them. He is still the consort of the Goddess, but his role is more for harvesting than for seed planting. This does not mean that the Sage aspect of manhood is devoid of sexual union, to the contrary, the creative urge or sex drive is stronger at this stage of life. It is just sublimated or channeled to the focus of the outcome instead of the chase.

The last sub-aspect of the Sage is the *Trickster* or the "weird little holy man." This aspect of the Sage is where the label "eccentric" comes from. At this stage of life a man knows what is really important in life and what really doesn't matter. What you take with you into the next incarnation is what is important. All the games of the ego are not important at all. This aspect of the Sage doesn't take the trivial problems of life too seriously. The old Sage uses laughter jokes and pranks to teach one to always look to the high echelons of things. His motto is, "if it is not going to matter in five years, then FIDO - forget it and drive on." Life is too short to sweat the small stuff. Always strive to be happy but never content.

When a man hears the call of the Sage and accepts it, his life energy is changed from an external focus to an internal one. He no longer perceives life as separate from his existence. It is as if he is not a man having a dream, but he IS the dream and controls it. This state of awareness can be achieved with the Rove and Father; however, the Sage has the power of endurance to live it unobtrusively in regards to the cycle of change that is necessary to the will of the Gods and nature. Hence is the blessing of the Sage. " *Gods grant me the patience and conviction to accept the things that must be changed, but when change is necessary, the strength and courage to see it through and the Sage's wisdom to know the difference.*"

81

Here is an explanation of the four tools of the Sage state and their associations:

The Stone: The Druids spoke of a blue holy stone; this might refer to what is known in Wicca as a Goddess stone, a stone with a natural hole through it. The stone of a Sage can be a stone or gemstone of any kind or size. It needs to be acquired by some form of personal sacrifice. The stone is the Sage's conviction, his confidence or faith, his "Rock of Gibraltar," so to speak. It helps him keep grounded in his intent. It symbolizes the rock of his foundation in his spiritual life. Its direction is north, the element of earth. Its associations are endurance, calmness, methodical planning, magical places, goal setting, mountain tops, midnight, the color black and the Law of the Magi - to keep silent.

The Staff: The staff represents the rod of authority, the power to lead and command magic. I have seen some beautiful hand carved staves and some that were designed by nature herself. The wood for a Sage's staff should be light wood such as willow, ash, birch, etc. Because this staff is used for magic not physical combat, it needs to be light weight yet durable.

The staff is the control the magician has of his thought world, his ability to focus and concentrate with clean intention. The mind is where all magic begins and where the attention goes, the energy flows. The direction of the staff is east, the element of air. Its associations are books, knowledge, charts, maps, power to reason, any school of learning, wind, clouds, winged creatures, dawn, the color red and the Law of the Magi - to know.

The Dagger or Athame: In Wicca, the black handled knife is the witches' tool of projection. The Sage's dagger can be an athame of any double edged knife or dagger. In some traditions, it is the sickle. The dagger is the magician's fire, his power to call forth action. His ability to create an image with such passion as to give it life. Using the living life force of his, own fire, he jump starts the image into existence in the higher realms. He causes it to move through the ether leaving behind a trail of electromagnet fields which swirl and begin to accumulate the substance of astral matter and give it manifestation. The direction of the dagger is south, the element of fire. Its associations are forging, burning embers, fast movement, courage, and the dragon's heart, glowing coals, noonday, the color of white and the Law of the Magi - to dare.

The Black Mirror: The black mirror is a scrying tool utilized to peer into the astral realm for clairvoyant vision. To the Sage it is also an instrument to travel to the astral world and contact his creation so that he can lead it back to this realm for physical manifestation. The black mirror is the doorway for the Sage into other worlds. Utilizing strong emotions and feelings about his magical goal, he seizes his intention and with his will to power pulls it into this reality. The black mirrors direction is west, the element of water. Its associations are rain, thundershowers, ponds, any water with surface tension, determination, fortitude, all emotional reactions, ducks, the color gray and the Law of the Magi - to will.

Sagehood can be a fulfilling time in a man's life if he accepts it. If he is in tune with the cycles of life and nature, he feels the joy and wonderment of the stage of manhood. Most men, however, resist the call of the Sage because they are misinformed of what is required to accept old age. The call of the Sage to a man is subtle. It usually occurs during what has been called the "midlife crisis." Because of our cultures warped ideas about manhood, most men think their manliness is in their virility.

When the time comes for a man to move from

the Father stage into the Sagehood they feel threatened. They are under the misconception that they have to give up part of their manhood. As stated earlier, the sex drive is stronger in the sage. Some men think you have to give up sex as a sage. This is anything but the truth. They start doing all sorts of crazy things in an attempt to hang on to their youth. Some men never recognize this time of transition and never internally accept it. They end up becoming grumpy old men that no one can stand to be around.

To help men understand and accept this time of transition of life, Witchcraft and Paganism honor those points of life with *Rites of Passage*. These rites assist the man to emotionally and psychologically accept the true meaning of manhood so he can become part of it instead of it being a part of him.

IX Rites of Passage

In our culture today the standard of living or way of life is set upon the forty to fifty years plan. When you graduate from school, you get a job or find an occupation that will provide enough money to supply you with the necessities to sustain life. This consists of things such as a home, automobiles, food, clothing, utilities, etc., as well as some pleasures also known as the comforts of life. Then you work generally eight hours a day, five days a week for the next thirty or forty years, at which time if you are lucky you have your home paid for and enough money in savings or investments to keep up the lifestyle without having to maintain your occupation so you can retire in comfort.

This is the outward focus of our lives. Within this focus we apply, when we find the time, the other values of life we cherish, such as love, family, religious affiliations or spiritual connections.

It seems that our internal values, our times of celebration, worship, intimate relationships and spiritualism are set around the outer focuses of the forty to fifty-year plan which has been called "earning a living."

As our computerized civilization progresses, it seems to make life more complicated. Maybe we need to take the advice of Henry David Thoreau, "Simplify, simplify, simplify." In the past century our society has been growing into this fast paced way of life. In the process, our culture has overlooked or forgotten the internal achievements of the self within, the human being as it progresses through life. Today only a small number of these life achievements are recognized and honored with rites and ceremonies, such as birthdays, graduations, weddings and funerals.

In Wicca and Paganism the internal growth of the self is honored and recognized with rites of passage. These rites help the individual understand and deal with the emotional, chemical and physical changes that they are experiencing during these times of transition. These rites are religious or spiritual in nature and may include rites such as birth rites, puberty rites, rites for first sexual experiences, Handfastings (Wiccan weddings), rites of libation, clergy rites, women's mysteries and men's mysteries to just name a few.

Since we are looking at Pagan Men in this book, let us examine some of the rites of passage for men. As stated earlier, the rites of passage are designed to bring about a psychological acceptance of internal and external growth of the individual as they progress through life. I am reminded of Alex Sander's statement, "Within the kingdom of your own body, shalt thou eat the bread of thine own initiation."

A few years ago, I had to perform the puberty rite, in some traditions called a "manning" for the son of one of my coven members. I had known and loved this boy since the day he was born. As the High Priest, I needed to talk and counsel with him a few days before the ritual to help him understand what was going to take place and the changes he was experiencing in this time of his life. I took him to a local coffee shop and sat in the back corner booth so our conversation would be more private. After a few minutes of small talk, I asked him how he felt about the upcoming ritual and if he knew what it represented. He said he was a little nervous and scared because the rite, to him, meant he was about to become a man and he didn't know what being a man meant. I told him not to worry that nobody expected him to act grown up, that puberty means you are entering the doorway to manhood, which is a transitional time for him and that he did not have to put away the child inside of himself. This rite merely recognizes that the child is growing up.

I asked him, "Do you know what the sign is for a young man coming to manhood?"

He said, "Well, I've got a few chin whiskers."

I laughed and told him that was one sign but as you know, women when they become capable of bearing children have an outward sign, the menstrual cycle, their monthly issue of blood. He knew that. I also told him with a man it is an inward sign. His eyebrows raised and he had a puzzled look on his face.

I looked him in the eyes and said, "As your High Priest for this rite, I need to ask you a question: Do you masturbate?"

He looked shocked and embarrassed and stumbles out a few, "Well...I...uhhh." I quickly said, "It is okay. I still masturbate." The look on his face became relaxed he was no longer feeling threatened. He calmly responded, "Yeah, sure." Then I asked, "Do you ejaculate semen? Because that is the inward sign of a man and if you do, you are definitely ready for this rite." It was like a light bulb went off in his head; he slowly started nodding his head in the affirmative and said, "I understand, Uncle Terry, yes I do." I spent the next couple of hours explaining to him the responsibilities, ethics and personal integrity he would be developing in the next few years of his life. He told me a few years later that his "manning" was a very deep, spiritual experience for him.

I am now presenting three rites of passage for reference, which we use in our church and coven. They are set to our tradition, but could easily be adapted to any tradition. The last is my own personal Sageing given to me at the May Day festival in Memphis, Tennessee in May of 2001. In keeping with the context of this book, we will begin with the Rove Rite of Passage.

I. The Rove Rite of Passage:

Items needed:
The four tools or weapons (the Shield, the Spear, the Sword and the Bow)
For the altar; horns or antlers, goblet of ale, two red candles, a small bowl of red paint (washable water paint)

The circle is set up with the four weapons in their appropriate directions, the Shield in the north, the Spear in the east, the Sword in the south and the Bow in the west.

The High Priest or Priestess gathers everyone into the circle. The dedicate Rove waits outside the circle. The circle is cast by the High Priest or High Priestess and the elements are called as follows:

Summoner: From the northern realm of Earth, do I call upon the power of the Shield. Hallow this place where we stand, bring us strength and protection. So mote it be!

Summoner: From the eastern realm of Air, do I call upon the power of the Spear.
Hallow this place where we stand, pierce our ignorance with knowledge. So mote it be!

Summoner: From the southern realm of Fire, do I call upon the power of the Sword. Hallow this place where we stand, slash through our inertia and move us to action. So mote it be!

Summoner: From the western realm of Water, do I call upon the power of the Bow. Hallow this place where we stand, take aim upon thy mark and let thy arrows fulfill our goals. So mote it be!

The High Priest and High Priestess invoke the Lord and Lady.

High Priestess: I call upon the Ancient Goddess, Badb, the battle raven, the queen who watches over warriors in battle. I invoke thee to witness now this sacred rite. So mote it be!

High Priest: I call upon the great horned God, Cernunnos, keeper of the forest deep, master of beast and sun. I invoke thee to witness now this sacred rite. So mote it be!

Summoner speaks: Hear ye! Hear ye! There comes one today that desires this rite of manhood. Let him now be brought before the Gods and the gathering.

A doorway is cut into the circle and the man is lead into the gathering and stands in front of the altar. The High Priestess asks the dedicate the following questions:

High Priestess: What is thy name?
The dedicate gives his name.
High Priestess: Do you desire the rite of manhood?
Dedicate: Yes!
High Priestess: By what authority do you claim this rite?
Dedicate: By the right of nature and the progression of life.
High Priestess: Are you willing to let go of the child inside of you to become a man?

Dedicate: No, I take the child that I am with me.
High Priestess: Very good!
High Priest: Know you this, to be a man you will be held accountable for your actions, words and deeds. Your honor and reputation are one and the same. Your honor is the only true measure you have, and your honor or lack of honor is how you will be remembered. Do you accept this?
Dedicate: Yes!

The High Priestess picks up the bowl of red paint and walks around the altar to stand in front of the dedicate.

High Priestess: By this rite of passage and by the power of the Gods do we now proclaim this man to be a Rove. She dips three fingers in the paint and swipes three marks across his left cheek and says: *I now give you the right and power of the lover.*

She dips again and swipes the right cheek saying: I now give you the right and power of the protector. She dips her fingers a third time and swipes the forehead and says*: I now give you the power of the hunter. Welcome my son into the Rove stage of manhood.*

High Priest: At this time when the air smells of raw

earth and the neck of the stag swells with the rut, when Herne the hunter is upon the wild hunt. This is the time of the Rove. The Rove yearns for conquest and battle, this feeling and this power surges through his blood. This is the power of the Rove. The Rove knows this power and dares to use it. He wills it from his very being. This is the Rove spirit, strong, free and unlimited.

All cheer and welcome the new Rove with hugs and gifts. At this point everyone stays inside the circle and sits down to talk and share stories and cakes and ale. Then the Lord and Lady are released and the elements thanked and released. The circle is closed by whatever system or tradition is utilized by the group.

II. The Father Rite of Passage

Items needed:
Loaf of bread
Chalice of tomato juice
20 or more common bricks, brickbats or blocks of wood
A knapsack or toe sack
Standard altar set up
Four tools of the father aspect set in the appropriate directions; hammer in the north, three-tined fork in the east, double-edged ax in the south, and cauldron in the west

The High Priest or Priestess casts the circle and the elements are summoned beginning in the north as follows:

Summoner: I call upon the element of Earth through the power of the hammer, grant us the ability to mold and shape our Magic. So mote it be!

Summoner: I call upon the element of Air through the power of the pitchfork, grant us the ability to choose wisely and focus our Magic. So mote it be!

Summoner: I call upon the element of Fire through the power of the ax; grant us the ability to ignite action to our Magic. So mote it be!

Summoner: I call upon the element of Water through the power of the cauldron, grant us
the ability to have compassion and love with our Magic. So mote it be!

High Priest: Old Ones, there is one among us who has heard the call of the father and wishes that right of manhood. Let him step forward and reclaim his right. The man walks to the front of the altar and says; I, _____ do now claim this rite of passage. High Priest: The father stage of manhood is one of responsibility and transition. Are you willing to undertake this ordeal?

The man answers, "Yes!"

High Priest: Are you willing to leave the Rove stage behind?
The man answers, "No, I take him with me!"
High Priest: Wise answer indeed, for the Rove becomes and grows into the father. The man is lead to the gauntlet. This is all the men and boys lined up in

two rows. The man must walk the path between them.
Each man or boy has one or two bricks.

High Priest: The father stage of manhood is the path
that leads to union with the Goddess. The father works
for the promotion of life, all life, not just his own. Are
you, _____, willing to take on these burdens
for the Great Mother and assist her with all of her
manifestations?

The man answers, "Yes!"

The **High Priest** hands him the knapsack and says:
*Proceed and walk the path of the father. The man walks
the gauntlet and as he approaches each man or boy
they ask him a question such as: Father will you teach
me?, Father will you help me?, Father will you feed
me? As the man answers each question, each man or
boy places a brick in his* knapsack.
*When he completes the gauntlet with his sack heavy
with weight, the High Priest and High Priestess are
waiting for him.*

*The High Priest takes the sack and explains the weight
of the knapsack symbolizes the weight of the burdens of
the Great Mother.*

High Priest: The Rove has given his life's blood in service to the Goddess. When the Rove's blood is mixed with the essence of the Great Mother, he is transformed into the father, her Consort.

He is then handed the chalice of tomato juice. He is told that the chalice holds the Rove's blood and that he is to mix his blood with the essence of the Mother, he is to pour the contents onto the earth. After he has performed this act the High Priestess steps up to him.

High Priestess: Welcome Milord, I have been waiting for you all your life. Join with me now so as to fulfill your destiny.

The High Priestess and the man perform the symbolic Great Rite with the chalice and the athame.

High Priestess: As the cup is to the Goddess,
Man: So is the athame to the God,
Both: And so conjoined they bring blessedness and manifestation.
The man dips his athame into the cup she is holding.
High Priestess hands him a loaf of bread and says: As the father you are now my manifestor. You are the bread of life for all your children, whether they be kith

or kin. Go forth and feed your people with your new found essence and power.

The man now passes out the cakes and ale for everyone in the circle. After this grounding, the circle is closed according to the tradition.

III. The Sage Rite of Passage

Previously I stated that this is my own personal Sageing rite of passage. When it was given to me there were not any recognized Sages in our community; therefore, my rite was performed by three recognized Crones of our community. This rite was performed at our May Day festival (Beltaine) in Memphis, Tennessee in May of 2001. There were ninety people in this Circle. At the time of this writing I have given the rite to four men in our community.

This ritual was written by a dear friend of mine and a well respected Crone in our community, Rev. Trudy Herring.

"In keeping with the Celtic tradition of the SDCW-ATC, we will recreate the journey to Avalon.

Terry's Sageing ceremony will be announced and all will gather in the ritual area. A circle will be marked out in votive candles and there will be three torches lined up behind the altar. On the altar will be tools and symbols of the Four Elements and the God. The Goddess will be represented by the Three Crones and the torches. Also on the altar will be a lantern, a blank book of shadows and Terry's staff."

The three Crones will be as follows:

The first Crone will represent the Crone aspect of the Crone. She will be dressed in purple (representing royalty) and wear a veil or crown. She will carry a staff.

The second Crone will represent the Mother aspect of the Crone. She will be dressed in white (representing healing). She will carry herbs.

The third Crone will represent the Maiden aspect of the Crone. She will wear black (representing mystery) and carry a sword.

Two ladies will represent the Maiden and will whatever they like, with flowers in their hair.

The assembly (with Terry at the rear) shall walk three times around the circle representing the journey to Avalon, while the Maidens and Crones set up the circle. Mother Crone will sing the circle into being and call up Avalon to be present. The Maidens will call the four elements. Maiden Crone will call the God and Crone will call the Goddess.

When all is ready, Terry should be at the East Quarter to enter the circle. The Maidens face him and the challenge is offered.

Maiden Crone: "Who comes to receive the ceremony of Sageing?"
Terry: "Names himself"
Crone: "By what right do you claim this Sageing?"
Terry: "By the right of manhood, by the right of life and by the rite of the Gods."
Mother Crone: "No man comes to the Isle of Women save by the hands of those women. Will you submit to their will?"
Terry: "Yes!"

The Maidens place a veil over Terry's head and lead him to the center of the circle where he kneels. Maidens stand four paces behind Terry. Maiden Crone takes the sword, points it at Terry and slowly circles him.

Maiden Crone: "Before, you wielded the sword of cunning and defeated your enemies. Will you now wield the sword of truth, tempered with mercy?"
Terry: "I will!"
She taps Terry on both shoulders: "Then strap on the

blunt sword of compassion. The sword you wield will be between your lips. Remember always your promise of today and speak always the truth, with mercy toward all."

Mother Crone: (circles Terry with hyssop wand): "Before, you ruled by virtue of your knowledge. Will you now rule with your heart, knowing all must end this life by death and each will stand in the presence of the Gods to state what they have learned?"

Terry: "I will!"

She places a bitter herb on Terry's tongue, saying: "Then eat of the bitterness of death, that you remember the sweetness of life. From your heart shall you teach, from your heart shall you rule! Remember always your promise of today and restore sweetness to the lives of all."

Crone (circles Terry with the Crone staff): "Before, your family was of your flesh, and of your blood. Will you now expand your family to include all who honor the Old Ones?"

Terry: "I will!"

Crone (giving Terry a chalice of blood red wine): "Then drink of the blood of those who honor the Old Ones that their blood becomes your blood, bone of your bone. Your family is now all who honor the Old Ones. Remember always your promise of today, and become father to all."

The three Crones take a cauldron from the altar and raise it up.

Mother Crone: "Mother to us all, you have heard the promises of the one before us. If it be your will, let him be revealed and drink from the Cauldron of Wisdom."

After 13 heartbeats, the Maidens come forward and lift the veil from Terry and he stands.

All three Crones: "This drink is given to you. Drink deep that the mysteries shall be revealed to you."
Terry drinks.

Maiden Crone: "This day have you become Sage and earn the right to walk among all the Elders. Take this lantern, that your light may be a beacon for all who seek wisdom."

Mother Crone: "This day have you become Sage and earned the right to teach all who seek wisdom. Take this book and write down all your experiences that all who wish to can learn from it."

Crone: "This day have you become Sage and earned the right to rule your children with the heart of compassion. Take this staff and rule wisely and walk among the Gods."

All: "Go in peace. Walk in beauty. Live in love."

Terry is lead from the circle by the Maidens. Terry leads the congregation to the hall while the Maidens and Crones close the circle.
The rite is ended.

Other Rites of Passage for Men

In this chapter I have also included some notable rites of passage that mark the progressive growth of manhood. These are written for group interaction but with a little adaptation they can be modified for solitary work as well.

I.   Manning (Puberty Rites)

The object of this rite of passage is to impress upon the boy that although he is still a child, he must begin to learn this lesson of life. One must become responsible for their actions and deeds. Throughout the rest of his life the law of action and reaction will exist. Whether it is right or wrong action is the lesson he must learn.

Items needed:
*The boy will need four gifts to give to the elements: a bone, a feather, a piece of coal and
a rose quartz.*
For this rite a series of torches should be set up in a zig zag pattern for the boy to walk.

The standard circle is cast, cleansed and consecrated. The four elements of earth, air, fire and water are summoned and the Lord and Lady are invoked. The boy is outside the circle standing at the entrance until the temple is erected.

The High Priest cuts a door in the circle and challenges the boy before entering the circle by saying: "It is better to remain outside in the darkness than to enter this circle with fear in your heart. How do you enter?"
The boy answers: "With perfect love and perfect trust."

The High Priest then escorts him to stand in the front of the altar.

High Priest: "Hear me Great Father. Witness now this rite. This young boy, with your acceptance, wishes to proclaim his rite of young manhood."
High Priestess (speaking to the boy): "Through the Great Mother from who's womb you came. Do you feel you are worthy of this rite?"
Boy: "Yes."
High Priest: Then in this hour let his presence be recognized by the four elements.

The High Priest leads the boy carrying his four elemental gifts, to each of the elements starting in the North, saying:

"Spirit of the North, Element of Earth, witness now the strength of this young man." The boy leaves *the bone* upon the northern altar.

"Spirit of the East, Element of Air, witness now the intelligence of this young man." The boy leaves *the feather* upon the eastern altar.

"Spirit of the South, Element of Fire, witness now the courage of this young man." The boy leaves the piece *of coal* upon the southern altar.

"Spirit of the West, Element of Water, witness now the love of this young man." The boy leaves the *rose quartz* upon the western altar.

The High Priest escorts him back to the center altar.

High Priest: "The Celtic warriors of old attained their worth by trials. _____ (boy's name), are you ready to face your challenge to gain access to the

gateway that leads to manhood?"
Boy: "Yes."
High Priest: "So be it."

The boy turns and faces the torches and is instructed to walk between the torches in a zigzag pattern then repeat the procedure and return to the center altar without getting burned. (It must be noted here that the torches can be of the tiki type with metal holders planted firmly in the ground with a least three feet of distance between them.)

As the boy returns to the altar the **High Priest** speaks:
"O Great God of Old, we call upon you, having witnessed this rite to accept this boy into the ranks of men. We ask that you bestow upon him the wisdom and responsibility of a man. This coven now delivers the young man to the Elders who will lead and teach him the ways of manhood. So mote it be!"
At this point, everyone welcomes the young man and if they have gifts for the young man, they are presented to him at this time.

The circle is now dismantled and closed according to the tradition.

II.   Rite of Mid-life

*This rite is given at the time of a man's mid-life crisis,
usually between the ages of 35 to 45 this rite is
designed to help a man to recognize that his strong
desire for change needs to be assimilated internally in
his being, instead of being forced externally in the
mundane world.*

The standard circle is cast, cleansed and consecrated.
The four elements of earth, air, fire and water are
summoned and the Lord and Lady are invoked.
The man is now named and called before the center
altar.

High Priestess: "O Gods of Old witness now and
recognize this man. He who has climbed the mountain
of consciousness and emerged on the other side. He
who has made the willing sacrifice and transcended
separateness."

High Priest: "On this day we honor (man's name),
who has taken the journey and vanquished the dragons
and monsters of fear and successfully found the grail,
the symbol of self."

High Priestess: "The mysteries promise that there is no contradiction or disharmony when life changes occur. Remember the bull is the father of the dragon and the dragon is also the father of the bull."

High Priest: "To accept changes in life as we grow older is a noble endeavor. You are awarded the title Zodion, a heroic symbol of nobility, represented by Aries and Taurus, for you have achieved the greatest of victories by conquering your self."

Everyone is invited to bless and congratulate the man. The circle is now dismantled and closed according to tradition.

III. Rite of Libation

*This rite is an attempt to blend the laws of the land in our culture with the ancient ways. It is performed on a man's twenty-first birthday. In most states in the United States, this is the legal age to buy alcoholic beverages. The lesson of this rite is **everything in moderation, nothing in excess.***
At the Southern Delta Church of Wicca ATC, we allow responsible drinking at certain events, but <u>no drunkenness or slobbery behavior.</u>

Items needed:
A small bottle of anointing oil
Alcoholic ale, mead or wine
Glasses for everyone in circle
A party can be scheduled for after the ritual

The circle is cast, cleansed and consecrated. The four elements are summoned and the Lord and Lady are invoked.

High Priest: "We gather here today for a celebration and recognition of <u>(man's name)</u> rite of passage of libation. There is a time for all things: to grow, a time to build and a time to explore. We welcome <u>(man's</u>

name) into a new beginning of life, with this rite of passage."

High Priestess: "You are now entering a new age of freedom and independence. But take heed, freedom is also accompanied by personal responsibility. Learn the lesson of practicality versus self-indulgence.

The **High Priest** picks up the anointing oil and as he anoints the man's forehead with the sign of the Celtic cross he says: "I anoint thee by the power of the Old Gods: giving you the ability to seek truth, judge for yourself and enjoy all that life offers you. Bright Blessings be always unto thee. So mote it be!"

The glasses are filled and passed to everyone in the circle.

High Priestess: "Salute to you (man's name). From this day forward upon your life's journey remember to thine own self be honest and true."

The circle is dismantled and closed according to the tradition.

X. In Harmony with the Elements

In ancient times the magicians believed that everything was composed of the four elements of creation. In Paganism, that belief is still honored today. The Elementals of Earth, Air, Fire and Water represent the four quadrants or directions of North, East, South and West respectively.

Everything has an association with one of the four elements. Each element is associated with a color and a metaphysical aspect. In some traditions each element is represented by entities known as spirits, guides or guardians. These elementals are an intricate part of ritual. Each element is summoned to the circle for added energy, protection or as witnesses to a rite. When you summon an element for these purposes, you are calling forth all of the associations of that element to manifest within yourself.

In Magic, the four elements are utilized and accessed through the old occult axiom of the four laws of the Magi. These laws are also known as the *Witches Pyramid.* It is basically a control system of energy flow, that witchcraft picturesquely calls "the spell of making"; each law represents the power to be summoned and controlled with the corresponding element. The four Laws of the Magi are: *"To Know, To Dare, To Will, and To Keep Silent."*

There are light and dark aspects to each law. The light aspects are considered to be the masculine force. The dark aspects are considered to be the feminine force. As we have already mentioned in chapter 4 these light aspects are projective. The dark aspects are receptive. An examination of this energy flow is necessary for the male witch to fully understand his role and his power in the "Spell of Making".

The first law of the Magi - *To Know* - represents the element of AIR. This is where the beginning transformation of all Magick starts. *To Know*, means knowledge, this is the intellect. The power of the mind, known as reasoning. Without knowledge, Magick has no focus. Like the wind in a slow breeze has the ability to carry itself around the world, gaining different perceptions and viewpoints of mother earth. It also has the ability to focus itself to a small area and pinpoint its power with three hundred mile an hour speed, such as a tornado. One expression *is receptive*, as in the breeze. The other *is projective*, as in the tornado.

To Know is to see all perceptions from all perspectives and then rationally make a decision as to what change needs to occur. This is where all Magick begins, in the mind with the element of air.

To Dare is associated with the element of fire. Once you have gained the knowledge of air, you then utilize the active force of fire. When a fire is lit, it consumes everything in its path. Fire is a living, breathing entity of its own. In the human emotions it is red hot passion it is the emotion of enthusiasm used to back up the knowledge of air with action. To Dare is to actually surrender yourself to a decision with passion. To take an idea from the mental realm and do whatever is necessary in the physical to manifest it. Borrowing from the TV series Star Trek's analogy, "To boldly go where no man has gone before," in performing the magical ritual.

Within the element of water, is where, *To Will*, resides. Water has the power when it is moving, such as a mighty river, that it will not stop. If it is dammed up, it will overflow. If anything is in its path it will wash it away, or rush around it. Rushing water will not stop until it reaches its destination. In the law of the Magi this is To Will. The magician's determination to accept unwaveringly, the decision to bring about manifestation. To actually *Will it* into being. This strong conviction is the very foundation of his belief or faith in the Magic. He fully understands the axiom, *"Faith is the substance of things hoped for; and the evidence of things not seen."*

To keep silent is the element of earth. The expression or outcome of Magic in the physical world. From the dark silent abyss of the subconscious mind, where it was un-manifested. It began its journey through the elements of air, fire, and water until it reaches manifestation in this corporeal realm. The power of the element of earth is to stand tall, solid as a rock. It is secure in it's foundation of its own existence, and doesn't have to explain, from whence it came. So it keeps silent and merely just IS.

According to modern Wicca this is how the power of the four elements are contacted and directed in a conjured circle. The attributes of the elements are accessed in the internal make up of the witch or magician and activated through the psyche. Then with specified intent the process is executed in a systematic order to bring about the desired outcome.

In other words through the law of magnetism, the positive image created in the astral realm of air, fills the negative void of manifestation in the corporeal realm of the earth. This is the *"Spell of Making"*.

Throughout the occult world associations have been attached to each element. These associations are supposed to assist the magician in personally relating to each element.

These correspondences may differ from tradition to tradition. For example, the Native Americans use red, black, white and yellow to represent the directions. Some people call the quarters from the North, others from the East. Some traditions call the North, Fire and the South, Earth. These are traditional correspondences for Wicca:

Element of Air
Direction: East
Colors: Yellow (white, pastels)
Energy: Projective
Keywords: *Birth, beginnings, learning, intelligence, reasoning, knowledge, wisdom, wishes, dreams, moving.*
Elemental: Sprites, Sylphs and Faeries
Time: Dawn
Season: Spring
Tools: Wand or staff, censer, incense
Zodiac: Aquarius, Gemini and Libra
Animals: Birds, Griffins
Places: Associated with high places, places of travel or of knowledge

Element of Fire

Direction: South
Colors: Red (crimson, orange and fuscia)
Energy: Projective
Keywords: *Life, heat, energy, will, imagination, passion, ambition, desire, courage, creativity*
Elemental: Imps, Fire Drakes, Salamanders, Dragons, Nagas, Lion and Phoenix
Time: Noon
Season: Summer
Tools: Athame, sword (forged in fire), candles, bonfire
Zodiac: Aries, Leo and Sagittarius
Animals: Dragons, snakes and lizards
Places: Dry, hot places, fires or places of fire and heat

Element of Water

Direction: West
Color: Blue (indigo, green, gray, turquoise)
Energy: Receptive
Keywords: Death, emotions, love, purification, sub-conscious, mystery, psychic awareness, intuition, dreams
Elemental: Mermaids, Undines, Nymphs and Pixies

120

Time: Twilight
Season: Autumn
Tools: Cauldron, chalice, cup
Zodiac: Cancer, Scorpio and Pisces
Animals: Fish, amphibians, aquatic mammals, water birds, sea life
Places: Bodies of water, wet, marshy land

Element of Earth
Direction: North
Color: Green (black, brown and earth tones)
Energy: Receptive
Keywords: *re-birth, nature, growth, prosperity, stability, strength, steadfastness, fertility and abundance*
Elemental: Gnomes, trolls
Time: Midnight
Season: Winter
Tools: Stone, Pentagram
Zodiac: Taurus, Virgo and Capricorn
Animals: Wild animals, any not belonging to the other elements, traditionally wolves, buffaloes, bulls, bears, horses
Places: Natural settings or formations such as mountains or forests, deep or hidden places such as caves

Some also consider a fifth element of which all things are composed. That element is Spirit. Spirit is the manifestation of all things.

Element of Spirit
Also called Akasha
Direction: All
Color: Purple
Keywords: *Spirit, life, centering, transforming*

One of the best things about being a man is our projective energy. We are good at it. But what about our receptive energy? Because we are born physically male this, at least, in the emotional and mental realms, keep us out of balance.

    Meditation is one good way to balance the projective and receptive energy within the male witch. Meditation calms one's inner being so as to be able to connect with the Goddess within. One of the best ways to accomplish this is to utilize the power of the four elements.

Meditation for the Elements:

It is important for men to become acquainted with the elements. They should be familiar with the energies they summon and work with and know what they expect from them. The following is a meditation exercise to help you become acquainted with the elements.

You will need a period of time when you are not going to be disturbed. It is also recommended that you conduct this exercise outside, perhaps in a park or your backyard. The idea is to allow yourself to become closer with nature and familiar with the elements.

Cast a small circle big enough for you to sit in and face the appropriate direction. If you are unfamiliar with casting a circle, there is an example of casting the circle for a new moon ritual in Appendix B of this book.

Sit and think about the elements and their associations. Spend as much time as you need to be comfortable and ready to continue. It is recommended that you take at least ten minutes.

When you are ready, begin in the North quadrant with the element of earth. Then say, "Element of Earth, who rules the North, I summon you to attend this circle, that I may know you better." As you finish, you should visualize a green mist swirling towards the edge of your circle. Take three deep breaths and imagine with each breath you breathe in the green mist and let it fill you with its calmness and serenity.

Enjoy the time you spend with this element and let its effects become part of you. When you are finished experiencing an element, dismiss and thank the element, then move to the next quadrant and element.

When you are ready for the next element, choose the appropriate direction and begin again. This time visualize the color and associations for the element you are working with. For example, if you are working with the element of Air, you would picture a yellow mist and perhaps, feel yourself drifting, experiencing a new beginning and/or wisdom. Consult the previous chart for other suggestions.

XI The Gods of Pagan Manhood

According to Carl Jung, all God forms are aspects of the archetypes of divinity, the inherent awareness of Deity. All humans have an unconscious knowledge or awareness of a divine power or force greater than themselves. The archetypes or god forms give the individual a channel to develop a personal relationship with a divine source. The druidic saying, "All Gods are aspects of the one God," follows this premise.

Throughout history, pagan cultures developed an archetypical link to the divine source that was associated to their heritage and culture. These are the God and Goddess themes portrayed through the pantheons from different groups of people around the world. Are all of these Gods sentient beings or merely forces of nature? That depends on which Witch you talk too. This is where the individual path comes into play in Wicca. "According to your belief, be it unto you," as the saying goes. The beauty of Wicca is, regardless of how many differing beliefs there are they are all correct. There is no one dogma of Witchcraft.

Men in Witchcraft should develop a personal relationship to the God force by spending time in meditation and communing with the Gods. Attuning to the God within through observance of the eight Sabbats not only aligns the man with a deity but also aligns him with the nature of the Earth Mother through the turning of the solar wheel of life. I have listed for the reader a few of the Gods that correspond to the three stages of manhood. This is not a complete list, but a few examples. The reader is encouraged to study other works on the Gods of Wicca, some of which can be found in the bibliography at the end of this book.

Gods for the Rove Stage:

Adonis: (Greek) Son of Cinyras, a handsome youth and keen hunter. So beautiful was he   that two Goddesses fought over him, Persephone and Aphrodite. He is associated with death and resurrection and the hunt.

Angus Mac Og: (Irish) Known as the young God of love and beauty. He had a golden   harp that when played, no one could resist. It is said that his kisses turned into birds that whispered thoughts of love into lover's ears.

126

Apollo: (Greek) The lover God because he had numerous affairs. He was also skilled in the musical arts. He is equated with the Greek maxims, "know thyself" and "nothing too much." He brings enlightenment, atonement and purification.

Cernunnos: (Celtic) The horned God usually portrayed with antlers. He is thought to have been the original God of the Hunt. He represents the wildness in men, the animalistic nature in fertility or virility. According to legend he was the blending of a man and a stag.

Finn: (Irish) Leader of the Fianna Warriors of Ireland. He was an expert hurler, swimmer, runner and hunter. He is associated with bravery, cunning, protection and wisdom. He gained his wisdom as a boy when he ate the salmon of wisdom foretold in a prophecy.

Horus: (Egyptian) A falcon-headed sky God that represents the struggle between life and death and the powers of light and darkness. He is said to have two eyes, one sun-eye and one moon-eye. In some stories he is Osiris' brother, in others Osiris is his father.

Lugh: (Irish) "The bright and shining one." One of the Tuatha De Dannan. He was made high king after he bested all of the champion warriors. Lugh is known as the God of war by most all Irish traditions. He is also equated as the Sun God. He had a magic spear that thirsted for blood. It was alive and could wield itself.

Pan: (Greek) Son of Hermes, he is part animal, part human, with goat horns and hoofs. He is known as the Shepherd's God. He plays the magical pipes or reeds. So sweet was his music he could charm any woodland nymph. In the Homeric Hymn he is called a noisy, merry God.

Tyr: (Norse) Asa God: "The One-Handed." He lost his hand in a battle with the wolf Fenrir. He is the patron of the thing or assembly. He is a Warrior God that oversees law, legal matters and victory in battle.

Gods of the Father Stage:

Belinos: (Celtic) The Sun God, God of light, also known as the God of health. After many battles with his brother Brennius, the God of death and the Underworld, he remained in England to build the Gate of Trinovantum on the banks of the Thames which to this day is called Billingsgate.

Bran: (Celtic) The son of the sea god Llyr. Known as "the Venerable Head," because he ordered his own head be cut off and buried at the White Mount of London. For eighty years it gave council and pleasant conversations to his followers.

Cuchulain: (Irish) Champion of War. Personification of the sun. So terrible was his wrath that when oppressed by his enemies, clouds with rain and lightening would form above his head. He is most famous for his conquest as a solar God, into the region of Hades or the underworld. Another one of his exploits as a hero God is in the Great War called, "Driving of the Cattle of Cooley."

The Dagda: (Irish) The "Good God," a God of the earth, he had a cauldron called "the Undry," from which none went away hungry. It always had food and nobody was unsatisfied. He is said to be the father of the Irish Gods. He was a formidable warrior and both a defender of his people and a nourisher.

129

Odin: (Norse) Chief of the Gods, Odin is a war God and magician who controls battles and gives inspiration. To rule the Asa Gods it is written that he drank the egg white mead of the Fountain of Mimir which cost him his eye. He is known as the "All Father, Sky God and the Great Father."

Osiris: (Egyptian) God of the afterlife and the God of Vegetation, King of Eternity. Osiris was all of these, revered in Egypt as Christ was to the Christians. Tradition says he taught the people how to plant and harvest grain, make bread and brew beer. He organized Egypt into a civilization.

Zeus: (Greek) Supreme Father God, King of Olympian Gods, Kronos, a titan and his sister Rhea. He rose to power after defeating his father, according to some traditions, and killing him. Zeus has several wives and a multitude of lovers: all bore him sons and daughters. His greatest battle to become master of the Gods was a fight with the monster Typhoeus. Zeus finally defeated him with his thunderbolts.

Gods of the Sage Stage:

Gwydion: (British) The druid of the Gods, the master of illusion and fantasy, Gwydion was known as the teacher of all that is useful and good and a helper to mankind. He fought against the underworld powers for the gifts they refused to give up. He is best known for the "Battle of Trees." In the underworld, he magically guessed the name of the invincible god Hades and broke the powers of darkness.

Hermes: (Greek) Messenger of the Gods. He is the God of intellect, travel and also a trickster, like Pan, his son, he is horned and goat-footed. Hermes also escorted dead souls to the afterlife. His Roman equivalent is Mercury.

Loki: (Norse) The Nordic trickster God. Quick-witted and cunning, Loki is one of the Aesir, the Gods and Goddesses who live in Asgard. He was originally a fire demon who developed into a benevolent God. Loki's cunning was often useful to his fellow Gods, he once shape-shifted into a mare and birthed a foal with eight feet, Odin's mount Sliepnir, which none could overtake. Loki represents constructive cleverness or cunning to dodge responsibility if taken selfishly.

131

Merlin: (Welsh-British) In some traditions, Merlin was half human and half God. In other myths he was a bard or druid. He could use magic and had the gift of the sight. The first writings about him were by Geoffrey of Monmouth in the 1130's A. D. According to the legends, Merlin was a wise old Sage who was interconnected with the Gods in promoting and keeping the sovereignty of the land and the people. His mission in his lifetime was to institute events in the lives of humans to propagate this sovereignty, hence his role in the legend of Arthur and the Knights of the Round Table.

Ossian: (Irish) Son of Finn, champion warrior of the Fianna and writer of the "Ossianic Ballads." His mother Sadb was changed into a deer which is how he got his name Ossian, which means fawn. One of the last of the Fianna to survive until the time of St. Patrick, he spent three hundred years in the "Land of the Young." When he came back to Ireland all had changed and St. Patrick tried to convert him. As a gray-haired sage he replied he would not believe in a hell or a God who would not be proud to claim the friendship of Finn. If this is not so, what is the use of eternal life with no hunting or wooing of fair women. He said he would go to the Fenians whether they sit at the feast or in the fire.

Gwyn Ap Nudd: (Welsh) God of the underworld, Lord of death and resurrection. Gwyn Ap Nudd is well known for his wild hunt with his demon dogs, for he hunts not for animals but for the souls of men. In the Black Book of Caermarthen there is a poem of which he is the subject. The last two verses are: "I have been where the soldiers of Britain were slain, from the east to the north; I am the escort of the grave. I have been where the soldiers were slain, from the east to the south; I am alive, they in death."

XII Consort of the High Priestess

There have been many aspects and sub-aspects of the three stages of manhood discussed in the previous chapters of this book including consort. The consort of the High Priestess, however, is a different and a very important aspect as well.

What does the word "*consort*" mean? Consort means companion or partner, to unite in company, associate. To gain a better understanding of what a consort is, we must first know what the role of the High Priestess is.

A High Priestess' role is not an easy one, nor always a fun one; however it is learning an enlightening experience. A High Priestess is often clergy, she is a guide for the people, a representative of the Goddess in her many aspects and mother to all. Therefore the work that she does is not just inside the circle. She is on duty twenty-four hours a day, seven days a week. It is for her, a way of life. She teaches counsels, researches, and studies and lives her path. She is an example to all her students, friends and community. She takes the brunt of the blows in most situations, as she is the creator. As it states in the Charge of the Goddess by Doreen Valienti, "*From me all things proceed and unto me they must return."* She is responsible for not only her spiritual path but for all those she guides and teaches. She is the focal point in the physical mechanics of a coven and the one to receive the accusations when things don't go as planned. These are just a few of the responsibilities of the High Priestess, the basis from which an entire series of books should probably be written.

The *Consort* of the High Priestess is a role that requires dedication and work. The man that takes the position is agreeing to all of the above statements as well as many more. He must be strong in his spiritual path and convictions. He must also have love, respect and compassion in his heart for his High Priestess. Her life he should defend before his own. He should be secure in his manhood and know his path matches hers. The *Consort* must be self-confident, but non-egotistical, strong-willed yet not unbendable, grounded without being immovable. He must walk the walk and talk the talk, live the life of a High Priest, sometimes as clergy but most of all as counselor and friend.

The *Consort* is usually an aspect that comes with the father stage of life. The time in a man's life when he has fine tuned the Rove and hunter to become provider, giver, teacher and companion. He has matured and attuned himself to nature's energy of life, death and rebirth to know life is what he chooses it to be.

As The Rove, he ran the gauntlet, fought the battles, tasted the fruits of sweet innocent love, has seen the beauty of life and watched the dawning of a new day. He experienced the thrill of the chase as hunter and hunted. He knows the sweetness of victory and the dread of defeat. Now he is ready to live as gentle lover, kind friend and master of his own destiny. Now he is ready to take the hand of the Mother and create new life in the world of beauty or chaos, for he knows both.

How do I become the *Consort*? When will I be ready? How do I know? These are all questions that come to mind when a man hears the call of the father and chooses to act upon it. For each man it is different, there is no set answer or time frame. Some men are ready at a very early age, with others it comes late in life. It is dependent on each man's spiritual awakening and physical maturity.

In ancient times, it was often at an early age, while in our culture it often comes later. The lifespan for men of medieval times was short, due to the battles and work of that time period. In our culture, however, lifespan have increased greatly and can be seventy, eighty or even up to one hundred years. Even in this culture, men still become physical fathers at an early age, however being a physical father does not necessarily mean a man is ready or even prepared for that stage of his life. Likewise for a woman, giving birth does not absolutely qualify a woman as being in the mother aspect of her life.

The *Consort* must be a man of wisdom, compassion, understanding, tolerance and most of all people skills. He must have the ability to communicate with the High Priestess as well as the members of the coven and society in general. He must be slow to anger and yet quick to protect and serve.

In a sacred circle, or ritual, the energy of the *Consort* is extremely important. The High Priestess represents the Goddess, the wheel of the year or the cycles of life, while the High Priest or *Consort* represents the God, the movement of energy and the spinning of the wheel. Most often the High Priestess will cast the circle and create the wheel while the Consort spins the wheel. If a Consort doesn't control the energy or spin the wheel, the manifestation cannot take place. He must be aware of the energy and know how to move it. Therefore the circle is balanced and flows like a mighty river.

The most important part of a *Consort* is to be an equal to the High Priestess. Each has their own roles to fulfill and neither is greater nor lesser than the other.

When they are equals, balance can be attained, whereas if one attempts to be above or over the other, the balance is shifted and chaos is evident. Creation is possible only when the male plants the seed inside the female and for this to happen they must be equal partners in all aspects, especially within a sacred circle.

This is especially true when group worship is being observed, such as working a coven or an open circle. The High Priestess and High Priest maintain the balance of the circle through the *Law of Magnetism.*

Every material object has a positive and negative pole, including the human body. These opposite poles are what constitute physical manifestation. Without this polarity all objects would cease to exist. If either end of the polarity pole was removed from an object the molecular structure would scatter into infinity.

The Magic circle is created by the High Priestess utilizing feminine energy, which is one end of the magnetic pole. The High Priest using masculine energy stabilizes the circle, which is the opposite end of the polarity pole.

This process takes place within the individual when working a solitary ritual. The *Law of Magnetism* operates through their conscious and sub-conscious minds. The solitary witch invokes the Lord and the Lady within themselves. In group work the High

Priestess is the external manifestation of the Goddess incarnate. The High Priest is the external manifestation of the God incarnate.

The difference between a solitary ritual and a group ritual is in the dispensing of the sacraments. According to Blacksun in his book, "The Spell of Making" the sacraments are anything that helps us commune with the Gods. The High Priestess and her consort's duties in group worship are to dispense the sacraments to the people within the circle. To reflect the sacredness in the universe around us the ritual leaders have to include their fellow human beings in that sacredness. To do that is to dispense the sacraments.

The Magick circle when created by the High Priestess is the Wheel of Life from the Goddess. The High Priest duty as her *Consort* is to turn that wheel. He accomplishes this by watching the energies within the circle and keeping them moving and flowing physically, emotionally, and spiritually. An understanding of the *Law of Magnetism* and how they flow through all of the realms assists the consort in his endeavors.

Have you ever played with bar magnets? Two bar magnets that were identical? If you ever have, you might remember that if you pushed one magnet towards the other, as they came closer together there seemed to be an attraction set up. They appeared to jump together and form a connection. If you then turn one of the magnets around and pushed it toward the other, it would chase the other magnet all over a table without ever touching it. This is because each bar magnet has a positive and negative end.

When you put the two ends of each magnet together and they attracted one another it was a positive end of one magnet and the negative end of the other magnet. When you turned one magnet around and tried to put them together, you were attempting to put a positive end with another positive end or a negative to a negative end, and they repelled one another.

In the Law of Magnetism opposites attract and likes repel one another. This disputes the old adage of "Like attracts like". In nature like does not attract like, only opposites attract.

When the High Priestess creates the temple by casting the circle she is manipulating energies and creating a positive image in the ethereal realm, utilizing her feminine energy. The *Consort* utilizing his masculine energy draws that positive image down, to fill the negative void that exists in the corporeal realm. Thus the Magick circle is brought from the Spiritual realm into the physical realm. In the Magick circle, the High Priestess and her *Consort* become as one mind

and one accord and like *"The Great Rite"* so conjoin
they bring blessedness and manifestation.

XIII The Warrior Aspect
The Warrior-Priest-Sage

"As the cool autumn breeze
Crosses the old man's weather-beaten face
He is still awestruck by the beauty of the rising of the
daybreak star of dawn
Many is the time he has preformed this sacred ritual
In solitude and peace
Now as he sits in his sanctuary
His mind fills with memories of battles of long ago
That he fought and won
He starts to stand
His old body tired with aches and pains from old
wounds
Doesn't move like it once did
But there is still a twinkle in his eye
And there is pride in his stance as he welcomes the
morning sun
As his gnarled hands rise to give praise
His feels the power surge within him
His heart swells with the deep yearning
For new conquests
The Rove energy swirls around him
His slowly begins to move and dance

Around the circle faster and faster
He jumps, leaps and spins
A war like cry escapes his lungs
As the cone of power peaks
When it is done he dons his armor
And stoutly marches over the hill
To gather his men and one more time
Lead them to victory."
By Terry Michael Riley

In the realm of Sociology, thought patterns formulate systems of conduct. The way men think creates belief systems, which in turn, affect their attitudes. Men by nature utilize projective energy from the God force. Women utilize receptive energy from the Goddess force.

Throughout history men have set up systems or ways of life within their social structures. These codes of conduct are based primarily upon man's gregarious urge or instinct, coupled within intellectual reasoning. Unconsciously mankind has tried to deny his animal heritage because we want to believe we are more advanced than the animal. The idea that we were still animals became an insult to our intelligence. We have within us all the urges and instincts of our animal

144

ancestors. The only difference between us and the animal is that they have no choice but to act on the urge while we, as humans, have the ability to act or not, we have the gift of choice.

Man's ability to think inwardly and to reason is why these social structures are formed. These systems exist from the highest, complex outward expression, such as world governments, to the simplest, as a coven or single family unit. As such there has developed within our culture two distinct classes or categories of men. These classes have existed at least since man started becoming civilized and possibly even before that time. Men fall under the categories according to environmental programming, their individual growth of consciousness and their karmatic ties from reincarnation.

The first category of men is the "*assimilator*". This type of man accepts whatever system he lives in as the only way. The culture he lives in is one of order and regulation. He believes that the rules have been set up for the benefit of everyone. His thought patterns are geared towards promoting his system of life the way things are. He is a traditionalist. His philosophy is "if it's not broke don't fix it." The *assimilator* tries to make everything new fit into his life style; if it doesn't, then he shuns it and possibly destroys it. He brings every experience into his being and molds it to shape the system. He knows that everything in his life has a set pattern according to the system, of how it should grow or be. The assimilator is a free thinker and entertains new ideas as long as it does not disrupt the system. The system is his foundation.

The second category of men is the "*conceptualist*." This type of man is an innovator, a visionary. The *conceptualist* wants to better the system, to improve it. He wants to change the system to his perception of perfection. He sees that some rules and regulations limit his freedom. Therefore, he challenges the system whether it is thought, action or beliefs. The *conceptualist* would rather expand the system to encompass more, yet retain its basic structure. He doesn't like to control or be controlled. He realizes the value of the system but also recognizes his perceived flaws of limitations within its structure.

When these two types of men, singularly or in groups, come into conflict with sufficient force, the *warrior aspect* of manhood emerges.

The word *warrior* has varying ideas and concepts attached to it. The standard image most men have of warrior is "Conan," "Red Sonya" or maybe "Crazy Horse." This image is often associated with a fighter or physical prowess. While this may apply to physical strength there is a lot more to the definition of warrior.

Gandhi, Martin Luther King Jr. and even Jesus were warriors, although they did not use violence. They stood and fought for a higher principle which they believed in.

Throughout history warriors have fought against one another for basically only two reasons. The first is self defense which is considered by most as justified. The second reason is a little more complicated and requires an act of judgment or virtue. When assimilator and conceptualist men, as warriors, fight against each other, it is because of **Change!**

Whenever there is an altercation between warriors it is because the aggressor is trying to institute or enforce a change in the mind, actions or beliefs in the defender. The defender is merely resisting the change.

It must be noted that both warrior and warring parties have made a decision concerning the virtue of the change in question. Is it positive or negative, just or unjust? Do I change or resist? The result of these changes brings about the conflict or war.

It is now necessary to define what the essence of a true warrior is. In making these choices the true warrior considers **his integrity**, which is the first quality of a warrior.

Warriors have high standards of a virtuous nature, an adherence to the highest standard of right. A warrior's integrity is based on their ideals and principles of an uncompromising nature. Without this kind of a code of values, a warrior becomes nothing more than a mercenary.

The second quality of a warrior that is most necessary is **courage**. The word is derived from the Middle English word, "corage" which means heart. In the movie Braveheart, William Wallace's uncle tells him, "Your heart is free, have the courage to follow it." Courage is the strength and fortitude to stand and uphold one's integrity with firmness and will in the face of hardships, dangers and fear.

The third quality of a warrior is **discipline**. A warrior has to have self control. Discipline, in this sense, is training that corrects, molds or perfects the mental faculties and character. A warrior gains wisdom through a system of disciplines of the body, mind and spirit.

Magick to a warrior is the power within. The power to make change occur through will. To make this happen the warrior will not accept the current situation. The warrior's path is a path of **action**.

The old definition of the word war is, "to make matters worse." When a warrior works Magick he knows he is going to war and matters may become worse.

When Gandhi took on the British Empire, for a time, the situation became worse before the change finally occurred.

When Scotland won their freedom from England, war had to occur. Things became worse before they got better.

This is the magic power of the warrior's path. It is to build up internal fortitude with enough conviction to withstand the onslaught of seemly invincible odds when making that change.

A warrior's path is often one of **pain**. However, to the true warrior, pain is not a negative thing. He understands that pain is weakness leaving the body. A warrior accepts his pain whether it is physical, mental, emotional or spiritual. Pain means growth and change is occurring.

A warrior must develop a different understanding of pain. He learns to channel it into a positive outcome instead of running from it. When pain occurs it is an opportunity to build strength or succumb to weakness. Often times the supposed pain may or may not exist in a situation, but our own unwillingness to suffer the possibility of pain makes us fearful.

A warrior fully accepts the Wiccan challenge,

"You have come to the Craft to learn, often learning requires suffering, are you willing to suffer to learn?" The letters in the word PAIN, to the warrior mean: "Positive Awareness In Negativity."

The final aspect of the true warrior is **subservience**. Throughout history warriors have been the protectors and defenders of their people, tribes, clans and culture. They upheld their cultural ideas and religious beliefs. To become a warrior was to pledge with blood, bone and heart (all that they were) to the continuation of their people's way of life. Some warriors like Joan of Arc, Gandhi and William Wallace took their commitments not only to their people but to the world and fought for ideals of justice and freedom.

When the vision leaves the mind and enters the heart, the true warrior energies form within. The difference between a soldier and a warrior is this: soldiers march but warrior dance.

My own rite of passage of the Warrior aspect came as a real life experience at the age of thirty eight in august of 1993. It was when I organized and led over one hundred Pagans in a Freedom of Religion March in Jonesboro, Arkansas.

The March gained worldwide notoriety in the media. This was not my intent when I organized it. The forced closure of our Occult Shop by some Christians in our town brought out My Warrior aspect to stand and fight on a principle. Freedom of Religion in this country meant to me, freedom of ALL religions in ALL areas of the United States. I felt that our area of the Bible belt needed to be forced into acknowledging that basic principle; whether they believed it or not.

By definition we, the Pagans, were the Conceptualist and our Christian opponents were the Assimilators. We were introducing and enacting a change of concepts in our community.

I would like to relate the story of our March to the reader from our Tomb of Lore, written by Shadar Stridenth, in the Bardic verse, which recounts the Warrior Spirit in us all.

" Marchant de Touta"

In the year of fire and flood, the lands of America were taunted by the shift faith. The Christians did preach of their end, their God and judgment day; and in so doing laid the grounds of this tale.

In the town of Jonesboro, a northeastern district of the land of Arkansas came the pleading shout of "Freedom." Not any freedom, but the most important of freedoms, the freedom of Spirit, and that was being denied and abused. The Spirit beckoned to be freed,

151

and the Touta Motani heeded the summons. Christian leaders had found a new target and we of the Motani were surely marked. The weapons of the Christians were the morals, doctrines and dogma of the Cowans and Motani was sorely attacked.

Terry {Graydove} bore heavily the results and wounds from these attacks; yet wounded and out-numbered. He was inspired to take the initiative and to turn the tides of this war. He spoke openly to the public of his rights as a citizen. He demanded his rights given by the laws of the land without persecution thereof. A just act it was, but woe unto Graydove.....

Iniashee, Graydove's wife, was keeper of a Shoppe. This shoppe was now the main target in Christendom, for not only did the Wiccan own and operate it, it was a Craft shoppe. One which had the ingredients and supplies of the Witch and magickal works.

Graydove, Iniashee, Syrus and Shadar together with some friends of Motani gathered about them the necessary tools of justice. With this they also assembled a mighty host to wield this weapon. And the Motani beheld the makings of a great army, tempered in truth and love, given to hope and peace, and guided by the laws of civil rights. The Motani, and Graydove now had the one weapon that would win this war, a host of truth;

and Graydove knew exactly how to wield it.

On Lughnasadh morning a gathering unlike any had ever seen began to take place in the quiet town. The Motani, The Wiccan Council, Pagan Alliance, and many more groups and solitaries assembled as one, in one voice, one mind, one body and one spirit. This day they marched on Christendom and the Christians beheld a mortal blow to their struggling power of the public viewpoint.

A merry host it was at the beginning, singing praises and chants, drumming and dancing as they progressed along. They chanted charms of protection and strength. Then came the protesting crowds. The law enforcement officers came not to stop the march, but to protect it. The chants became vibrant, they invoked civil rights for all, and the protesters were swayed momentarily to quietness; and the law officers walked proudly along.

The charms of the ancients we did sing and the power flowed as a raging torrent. The Christians in one last flurry began their simple magicks; yet naught came of their words nor works. The law officers drew in closer and became a living shield blocking the Christians and opening the desired path of the marchers.

As Graydove topped the last rise between us and

the final destination, the County Courthouse, the fleeting final act of the Christians became clear. They had erected a great cross and a massive crowd, and unto us they began songspells of their faith. They had taken to the field the full armor and armaments of Christianity.

A pause came upon the march, but it was merely a pause of moments, for we used it to guard our spirit against the Christian host. A pause taken for granted by the Christians who saw it as a victorious move by them, and a weakness of our people. Alas, a pause that allowed the law to take sides and it was our side that the law protected.

Likened to a great machine, the law officers began to reposition themselves. They took the point and reinforced and divided the Christian mass; as well as forming ranks to protect our flanks from any assault. We of the march followed in suit in our maneuvers. Greydove, as well as the pagan elders formed a frontline of strength and power. Drummers and chanters paired and began songspells of defense and inspiration. The host of the march tightened in together, and in one accord, stepped forward casting about them the law, and truth surrounded in spirit.

The Christian ranks fell away broken apart, was still holding to small groups to this side and that, but the march continued and passed by unswayed and unyielding. And what a sight it was!

To the courthouse the marchers proceeded and there it was that Graydove stood high and proud for he knew that Christendom had been defeated by the one thing they could not withstand...TRUTH.

It is our laws of the land that guarantees our religious and civil rights, to all regardless of their beliefs. It is in our religious laws and ordains that enable us to have an open mind and heart to all, even when we don't agree with others in their faiths. It is tolerance of all that allows our spirit to exist and become one with all of us. It is truth, a certain truth tried and tested by endurance that love is the law and the spirit is its keeper. And we are the keepers of the spirit. So mote it be!--------by Shadar Stridenth

XIV The Healer Aspect

The Healer aspect of man operates through all the stages of manhood. Many stories, myths and legends have been told and written about great healers. Throughout history healers have alleviated pain and suffering from their patients; some through the physical, some through the mental or emotional and some through the spiritual realm; some great healers have worked through all four systems. But what does it mean to heal, to be a healer?

In the dictionary, to heal means "to restore to original wholeness or integrity." So by that definition anything that is repaired is considered healed. The reason I mention this concept is because most men in our culture do not consider themselves as healers unless they are in the medical profession. But isn't an auto mechanic who repairs your car a healer? Isn't a farmer who tills the soil every year replacing minerals and nutrients to make it more fertile, actually healing the land? By this perspective, all men are healers of something.

Doctors, shamans, medicine men and native healers are people who innately tap into the protector aspect of the God and utilize the consort aspect to help restore the Goddess within, back to wholeness in the human body. Complete healing has to be done through the four fold nature of man. That is the spiritual, emotional, mental and physical being. This is accomplished by learning and applying the laws of life that operate through our systems.

Allow me to explain. There are four natural laws to the physical body. If these are not transgressed, the body will manifest health. These laws are:

1. **Nutrition -** The body must be fed the proper minerals and proteins to sustain proper condition. A balanced diet must be adhered to. The proper proportions of meats, vegetables and starches must be consumed in balanced amounts. Too much of anything is detrimental to the normal functioning of the body.

2. **Sanitation -** This states the body must be kept clean, outside and inside as well. Over a period of time, poisonous toxins build up in the system. The body needs to be flushed at least once a year through fasting.

3. **Movement -** All joints must be moved daily. Not exercise but rather movement to the point of a small amount of tiredness. The law states that inertia causes rust and disinclination to action.

158

4. **Rest and Recuperation -** The body is subject to the law of rhythm. There is a time for action and a time to relax. The body functions in cycles. A time to rest and relax must be adhered to on a daily basis.

When all four laws of the body are obeyed the expression will be healthy. If one law is transgressed and the other three obeyed there will be dis-ease in the body. Sometimes the physical ailments might manifest due to a mental or emotional block. Since being in the occult, I have learned that the magical adage, "As it is above, so shall it be below" attunes us to the knowledge of what is spiritual can and will find its ultimate expression in the three lower systems of the human being. Spirit is constantly molding matter and consciousness to form a vehicle for its expression. Depending on our choice, through our mental and emotional realms, regulates that expression to be positive or negative to us.

It must be noted that in the mental and emotional realms a direct link is connected to the five physical systems of the body. These five systems of the body are exactly corresponded to the five primary urges that were discussed in earlier chapters of this book. Therefore, when an emotional upheaval occurs in the physical, it activates one or more of the primary urges and throws it out of balance and causes that system of the body to manifest disease in the body.

For Example: Let's say that you didn't have the money to pay your rent and you begin to worry about losing your home, worried about being kicked out on the street. The worry that stems from fear is directly connected to the self-preservation urge. The chemical changes that take place in the body because the urge and the emotions are telling the spirit that a fight or flight reaction is called for. The self-preservation urge is cranked up into high gear or in other words, on the "high" side of operation. This urge has a direct influence over the digestive system of the body in expression. Therefore, when the digestive system is thrown out of balance, it doesn't function normally. By this example it is stressed or overworking to the high side, because of the supposed situation of a possible threat to the self-preservation urge. This was activated by the emotion of fear. At this point, the body would manifest an upset stomach, gastritis or heartburn, all because of worry. Even more serious conditions could develop such as ulcers in the stomach over a prolonged period of time.

To help a healer understand this connection between the urges, emotions and body systems here is a list of the primary urges and their corresponding associations:

1. **Self-preservation -** This urge influences the digestive system of the body.
2. **Self-expression -** The self-expression urge influences the eliminative system of the body.
3. **Creative urge or sex drive -** This urge influences the nervous system of the body.
4. **Will to power urge -** The musculature system of the body is influenced by this urge.
5. **Gregarious or herd urge -** This urge influences the circulatory system of the body.

Law: A statement of order or relation of phenomena, that so far as is known is invariable under the given conditions.

One only has to examine the universe in which we live to realize it is operated and governed by law and order. From the smallest bit of molecular structure to the highest metaphysical existence, everything is regulated by law…"Natural Law". By natural law, we do not mean, just physical. Natural law encompasses and operates through all the realms of existence: corporeal, astral, and ethereal.

These laws are set down by the All- Spirit. They cannot be broken. To break a law means it no longer exists. These laws can be transgressed but they continue to operate. When any of these laws are transgressed there is always reciprocation ensued to balance the transgression. In other words, unlike man made law like jurisprudence, for example where you might transgress and run a stop sign and get away with it. Natural law always has a price to pay for the transgression.

To be a healer one must of necessity undertake a close study and observation of the laws of life set in order and motion by the All-Spirit. The belief is if one fully understands and obeys these laws, it puts one in closer communion with life itself. Here then are the laws of life beginning with the eight universal laws.

1.) ***The All-Spirit IS*** : This is the one great law. As stated in chapter 2, the All-Spirit is everything in manifestation. Everything is an extension or expression of the All-Spirit. The All-Spirit Is Energy. Everything that exists is made up of different levels of energy. The All-Spirit is the electron within the atom. All electrons of all atoms according to science are identical. Therefore they are in everything, everywhere and they are constantly in movement. Ergo: Energy or the All-Spirit IS.

2.) *The Perpetual Transmutation of Radiant Energy:* This law stipulates continuality. Nothing is ever created or destroyed. There is merely transmutation of many levels. We live in an ocean of motion. Nothing is at rest. Everything is at a constant state of change from growth to decay and from decomposition into growth. There is no such thing as inertia. Everything and everyone is a whirling mass of electrons, protons, and neutrons.

Scientists tell us that our universe is expanding and has been since its creation. Compare this law to a pebble dropped to the center of a pond. It creates waves that roll to the outer edges of the pond. When the waves reach the edge they then flow back to the initial center to repeat the process over and over into infinity.

3.) *The Law of Vibration:* Starting at the molecular level again everything is at a certain rate of vibration; everything and everyone is sending and receiving vibes from the lowest form of solid matter up through the spectrum all the way to thought waves.

What separates the physical realm from the spiritual realm is a vibratory light line. The speed of light is over one hundred and eighty-six thousand miles per second. Anything that has a rate of vibration below the speed of light is perceived by our five physical senses. Anything that has a rate of vibration that is above the speed of light is not picked up by our physical senses. This does not mean that just because its vibration is above the speed of light that it is not real or have physical manifestation. It is just that we cannot hear, see, smell, taste or touch it.

A fire log is a good example of vibratory rate change. As a log it has a certain rate of vibration to exist in its current form. When it is set on fire its vibratory rate is changed and its form is transmuted into ash and smoke. But it was not actually destroyed. The image and label we put upon it was merely changed.

4.) *The Law of Relativity:* This law states that everything is related and dependant upon the relationship of everything else. Science has proven there is transference of electrons when objects come near one another in all forms of matter. This includes all realms even the ones made of higher forms of matter.

5.) *The Law of Rhythm*: The entire cosmos is set on cycles of rhythm. Like a pendulum swinging left and right. From the ebb and flow of the tides, to the rising and setting of the sun and moon, even the cycles of the seasons. All objects and things are subject to the law of rhythm.

6.) ***The Law of Polarity:*** We live in a world of opposites. The Law of Polarity states, for every Positive there is a Negative. For every front there has to be a back. For every Up there is a Down. Opposites are merely extreme ends of the same thing. This applies to the physical, mental, emotional, and Spiritual realms.

7.) ***Law of Cause and Effect****:* The Law of Cause and Effect proves, for every original cause in any realm, there has to be an effect: and for every effect there has to be an original cause. This law has been labeled causative continuality: because when an original cause becomes an effect, that effect becomes another original cause to produce another effect. This law gives credence to the theory of reincarnation and karma.

8.) ***The Law of Gender****:* Everything in the universe has masculine and feminine energy within it; the male aspect being projective, the female aspect being receptive. Within the atom of matter the nucleus is classified as masculine and the electrons classified as feminine. All things are under the Law of Gender.

The Emotional Laws: "I think, therefore I am!" this is a powerful, magical statement that is at the heart of human awareness. We humans innately want power. Self imposed power to get or manipulate the forces that exist so as to change or to bend them at our will. Why, because of our feelings. Psychologists say we as humans are ninety percent emotion and only ten percent intellect. Every decision we make is an emotional one. Emotions operate through the mind and the soul. Each choice that we make is either from the mind or from the soul. Emotional decisions of the mind are in resonance with the Ego. Emotional decisions of the soul are in resonance with the Higher Self.

These Emotional Laws dovetail and correlate with the eight Universal Laws. They are the extreme opposite ends of the same vibration with varying degrees in between. The emotional vibrations do extend an effect all levels of existence. Here is the list of the Emotional Laws of the Mind and the Soul:

Laws of the Mind:
  Fear
  Worry
  Anger
  Greed

Jealousy
Envy
Gossip/Slander
Egocentric
Cowardly
Prejudice
Lazy
Vengefulness
Deceitfulness
Impetuous
Hatred

Laws of the Soul:
Faith
Hope
Serenity
Charity
Trust
Contentment
Kindness
Altruism
Courage
Tolerance
Responsible
Forgiveness
Honesty

Patience
Love

To be a Healer is to understand ourselves. How we operate, not just physically but emotionally, mentally and spiritually as well. Before the medical profession was dominated by men in history, the woman was always consulted as the healer, mainly because of their intuitive nature or maybe because they seemed to have more compassion for the patient due to women's mysteries of birthing and midwifery. It wasn't until the eleventh or twelfth century that men really took a deep interest in healing.

As the field of medicine expanded and grew, it concentrated on the outer expression of illness and tried to conquer disease from the outside in. This was due to men's linear thinking process, which is how men's perspective tends to view things and situations. When men use their intuitive nature and listen to the Goddess within they become great Healers, utilizing the power of the God and the Goddess.

XV The Priesthood

Modern Wicca has opened the doors to Witchcraft by promoting self dedication and initiation into the Craft and the religion. It has been stated that all practitioners, once dedicated, are in fact priests and priestesses. This was not so in the old ways.

First, let's look at the definition of the word *Priest*. According to the Webster's Dictionary, a *Priest* is one who is authorized to perform the sacred rites of a religion. Now what are those sacred rites in Witchcraft? Is it the Lunar and Solar rites? Where does one get the authority to perform these rites, from the Gods, from oneself, from a coven or church?

Throughout history there have been priesthoods from many religious orders, each one having a different set of sacred rites according to their culture. Unless they were a secret order, they usually had a liturgy, a set of rites for public worship. To be a *Priest* or P*riestess* meant that an individual went through training to learn to dispense the sacraments through the performance of the liturgy, which was set down by the group, sect, order, coven or church. A Priest or Priestess had to be able to dispense the sacraments to the people. He or she assisted helping others to feel uplifted and have a genuinely spiritual experience. Often times, this training took years or even lifetimes.

There is a difference between being a *Priest* and being *Clergy*. Since we are dealing with the male perspective in this book, let's look at what it takes to be a *Priest* of witchcraft.

A man would have to have a deep desire to sincerely want to help people, all people, attain their own personal connection to their spirituality. Years ago I was working in a factory. Everyone in my home town knew that I was a witch. A week after I started to work a man began asking me questions about Wicca. He was a Baptist and wasn't interested in becoming Wiccan but was interested in what Wicca was.

As we talked over a period of time, we became friends. He would talk to me about his church, his wife and how he didn't understand a lot about the interpretations of the bible. I would explain to him what certain scriptures meant by my interpretation. I would counsel with him when he and his wife were having problems. One day, we were out in the yard working and he looked up at me and said, "You know Terry, I have learned more about my faith and become stronger in it by talking to you even though you are a witch. Why is that?" I told him if I had helped him in his path of spirituality then I had done my job as a priest.

Being a priest is about caring about people as well as the earth and the Gods. They are connected in this thing we call life.

In the old days, the religion was sustained and propagated by covens, small groups of six to thirteen people. Today, Wicca is one of the fastest growing religions in the United States. Legally recognized churches of Wicca have been established to meet the needs of the people. Most of the groups have public rites and liturgy to introduce newcomers to the Craft. The priests and priestesses of these organizations are clergy. They have dedicated their lives to the service of the Gods through their church or group. Many of these groups have adopted a set of Ordains, a code of ethics and laws that they live their lives by.

One of the first steps for men to become a priest is to learn to control the ego or shadow self. With men being projective by nature, this is not an easy task. Christ, Buddha and Gandhi were great Magi who lead thousands of people to higher consciousness, not with brute force but with gentleness and understanding.

Another aspect of priesthood that most overlook is sacrifice. It must be emphasized that we are referring to Wiccan/Pagan clergy, not to the modern concept that everyone is a priest or priestess of

Witchcraft by self-acclimation. We refer to those who have taken years of training and have dedicated their lives in service to the larger Pagan community and to the Gods.

The meaning of sacrifice can be compared to the definition of the rune *Gebo*, in the Norse divination system. It means, that which must be given up in order to gain spiritual wisdom. This is especially true when one decides to be Clergy-FOR THERE IS NO FREE LUNCH!

In times past the small coven met the needs of the people. Most covens consisted of seven to ten members with one or two students in training, because it took years to train a *Priest* or *Priestess* to third degree.

If one researches the scattered history of Witchcraft back through the years, you will find the basis of the religion in Druidism. The Druids were the priesthood of the Celtic people. The Celts were followers of the old religion and the Druids were their priests, healers, historians, diviners, judges and magic workers. According to some authors, Modern Wicca has it roots in Druidism. The Druid's had three levels of attainment in their teachings, the bard, ovate and druid. It took twenty years of training to become a druid. It has been suggested that some did not finish the training and quit at the ovate stage. From these second level druids the religious practices of magic evolved.

To be Clergy is to be *in servitude to your Gods, to nature and to the people.* This becomes a primary goal of your life and existence. Anyone and everyone can be a practitioner of the old religion, however, to be Clergy is a choice that very few make.

Make no mistake; I am not degrading or discounting self-initiation as not being valid. One's personal spiritual dedication to their chosen path is at the heart of paganism and Wicca. After all, remember the words of Alex Sanders, "Within the kingdom of thine own body, shalt thou eat the bread of thine own initiation."

Today there are a great many churches of Wicca and Paganism established and operating primarily to make the old religion more accessible to the new seeker. And yes, I have heard the argument that Paganism or Wicca will become an organized religion like Christianity. Well, let me ask this, "Where did the Christians get their structure from?" Weren't the Druids organized? How about the priesthood of the Temple of Delphi? What about the Tibetan and Buddhist monasteries or the Shaolin temples and their clergy? They were all operating and working structures of organized religion long before Christianity. The Christian Church only copied the Pagan structure to promote their faith. The same way they copied everything else from pre-established religious organizations.

So the Old Religions needs to be re-instituted with their sacred places and temples and let those who knowingly and willingly sacrifice their daily lives, train and become clergy to the land and the people.

Modern Wiccan/Pagan priesthood is different than clergy. In a lot of covens, there is a degree system to the Priesthood. The ritual leaders are called the High Priestess or the High Priest. These people are usually third degree initiates. The first and second degree levels are training levels for future leaders. Each coven governs themselves, teaching and training their traditions of the Craft, through initiations into the Mysteries. Whereas the Pagan Church accepts solitary practitioners and covens to their open public rites to make the Old Religions more accessible and assimilate information to the general public; this often times is a full time job and the people who dedicate their lives to this path and different organizations are the Clergy. Most say they are called to this path by their Gods.

So whether you choose to be a solitary practitioner, work in a coven, lead a coven or is Clergy all are valid and needed. The beauty of Paganism is there is a place for everyone that fits the individual's path to spirituality.

XVI Magic for Men

In most of the old grimories or magical text Magic has been called, "The Airts". This is appropriate considering to properly perform Magic it is an art form, which requires a lot of practice. So far in this book we have examined and discussed the power of the male witch. That was the intent of the work. We feel that in discussing Magic it would only be fair to state how the Airts are preformed by men and women. So as not to offend either gender we will be looking at the process objectively.

When men work Magic the internal process has to be viewed differently than the internal process when women work Magic. That is not to say that one way is better or more powerful than the other. They are just merely different.

As stated through this entire work men are projective, women are receptive in nature. They are each one end of the polarity pole, or one half of the whole. When a man and woman work Magic together, the two half's combine to form the whole. They complete a circuit of positive and negative energy. When one performs solitary Magic, that same balance has to occur within the individual.

This is accomplished, as stated in chapter three, through the conscious and sub- conscious mind; the God within, and the Goddess within, respectively.

The problem then is feelings. How do men feel the Goddess within and the women feel the God within them? How does a man tap into the feminine energy inside himself, when he is primarily feeling and utilizing masculine energy? The same problem is true in women only in reverse. How do they feel and tap into their masculine energy, when they are primarily feeling and utilizing feminine energy? This balance within the magician, whether male or female, has to take place in the art of Magic. Then have to complete the circuit.

In Wicca this is supposed to take place with the invocations of the Lord and Lady. If a true invocation were to occur with a male magician we can imagine a man standing in his ritual and after invoking the Goddess feels within his internal make up, like a woman. In a lot of men that would scare the hell out of them. This process is similar to shape shifting in many occult practices. The same process holds true for women invoking the God.

Physiologically speaking; the man has to give up his origination, and become subjective. A woman on the other hand has to give up her subjectivity and become originative. This process is achieved through auto suggestion and basic hypnosis.

Hypnosis, the word comes from Greece, and is derived from *Hypno*, the Greek god of sleep. It is a technique used to induce trance like states, or altered states of consciousness using suggestion.

The discovery of hypnosis dates back to 1775 with an Austrian physician named Franz Anton Mesmer. Mesmer believed there was a power similar to magnetism that influenced the human body. He called this power animal magnetism.

Doctor Mesmer developed a technique to induce a trance like state in his patient to cure them. This technique was called mesmerism. The mesmeric trance is today identified with the condition known as induced somnambulism in hypnosis. To under stand the trance like states in hypnosis it would be helpful to compare them to the electrical rhythm of brain waves. This is beneficial to men and women when working Magic.

Levels of consciousness in the brain are measured by the frequency of brainwaves. Normal waking consciousness in the human experience is called Beta level of awareness. At this level brainwave frequencies are measured at thirteen to thirty cycles per second.

When we are in a wakeful relaxed state such as meditation the brain is in the Alpha level of awareness. Here the brainwave frequencies are measured at eight to thirteen cycles per second.

During sleep or the unconscious level of awareness the frequencies of the brain waves are below six cycles per second. This is called Delta level of awareness.

When the hypnotic trance is induced, through suggestion, the brainwaves shift from Beta to Alpha levels of awareness. This state of trance is called Lethargic in hypnosis.

The second level of trance is called Cataleptic. It is a condition of suspended animation and a loss of voluntary motion. The brain waves are operating at seven to eight cycles a second in the Alpha level of awareness. Somnambulism is the third level of trance in hypnosis. It is and abnormal condition of sleep in which the motor acts "as waking" are preformed; other wise known as, sleepwalking. The brain waves are operating below six cycles per second in the delta level of awareness.

Therefore in a Magic ritual, a true invocation occurs, when the magician achieves the cataleptic state of trance; where by his or her origination is suspended and the personality of the God form assumes control of the consciousness. The magician is aware of what is going on and retains some control in the cataleptic trance, but if he or she relinquishes all control they will slip into Somnambulism and have no memory of the experience. In many different religions this is classified as a possession, a psychological state, in which an individual's normal personality is replaced by another.

The solitary magical ritual is designed so that either a man or woman can achieve this state and there by create balance in them, so that they can work Magic with a high degree of success. This is the total effect of what has been called in Magic, "To Conjure".

From the minute that the magician decides to perform a ritual, the act of conjuring begins while he or she is gathering tools and setting up the temple area the intent or purpose of the Magic is striking at triggers in the subconscious mind. The auto suggestion has already begun before the ritual is ever performed.

All the tools, robes, incense, altar etc. utilized in Wiccan rituals, are symbols of higher attributes to the magicians unconscious. As he or she goes through the process, of performing the ritual, a form of self hypnosis takes place. So they can achieve the altered states of consciousness to actually work the Magic.

It takes time for a would-be magician, to study and learn the various symbols used in magical ceremonies according to traditions or religions. Plus these symbols have to be assimilated into the unconscious portion of the magicians mind. This is the part of the law of the magi, discussed in chapter ten, as, TO KNOW.

After this is accomplished, it is then a matter of practice, practice, practice. Aleister Crowley, the most well known magician of the twentieth century, put it aptly when he said," to be an accomplished magician, one has to conjure often".

We cannot attest to the accuracy, but one report stated that Crowley was so powerful that on a clear sunshiny day, he could conjure a violent thunder storm with nothing but a sword and incantations.

By examining this information we can now see how the art of Magic operates through men and women's internal makeup. Although the energy is channeled slightly different in the gender expression, balance can be achieved. There by creating the positive and negative flow of energy to complete the circuit of magical manifestation.

In talking about Magic it would be un-just not to mention another aspect that is absolutely necessary in the performance of the Arts, and that is belief.

To understand how belief works in our Magic we have to give thought to thought itself. As Buddha said long ago, "All that we are is the result of what we have thought."

Everything we do or say is preceded by a thought impulse. Our thoughts predominate and determine our character and every aspect of our lives. "What the mind can conceive and believe, it shall achieve." In the words of Shakespeare, "There is nothing either good or bad, but thinking makes it so." The power of thought is that; it is a creative force and it controls the tempo of the mind. This draws the subconscious forces into play, and changes everything within and without.

Thoughts when they are repeated over and over become habit, A habit of the mind. When they are repeated often enough they become a suggestion to the subconscious. Once a thought is accepted into the subconscious not a power in the universe can stop it from manifesting.

That is why the study and practice of Magic is so important. Just reading a couple of books and doing a few rituals does not make one a magician. It is a life time work. Remember the words of the master adept, *"According to your belief; be it unto you."*

XVII Animals and the Gods

The relationship between humans and animals has been intertwined and a part of nature since life first began on this planet. As humans become more civilized and self aware, terrestrial and fantasy creatures came to symbolize the metaphysical powers associated with the higher realms.

The male Gods of most myths and legends are usually depicted with unique characteristics. In various cultures around the world, these stories have been passed around from generation to generation. Until the discovery of the written word these legends were passed on orally.

In most of the descriptions of the Gods they were associated with certain animals. In olden times these animals were seen as having magical, masculine attributes. These attributes were associated and attached to the male Gods so as to portray these same characteristics to men as totem animals.

A look at some of these animals and their attributes might help us understand our cultural programming about manhood.

A list of the most common animals related to various Gods in different cultures is presented here along with a list of gods and the animals associated with them.

Animals associated with Male Energy:

Bear: The strength and power of heavens is usually the symbolization of the bear. There are many stories of humans turned into bears and bears as Gods. The constellation of the big dipper, know as Ursus Major, the great bear has seven stars that are representations of the seven rays of the divine. Bears are known for the speed reaching thirty to forty miles per hour. They are also linked to trees which associate them with the world tree in most occult practices. There are "BEAR TREES" marked with claws as sign posts. Bears have always been at the top of the food chain eating almost anything.

Beetle: In Egypt the significance of the beetle was that it symbolized the solar gods and new life. The beetle was known for its practice of taking a piece of dung and rolling it into a ball, from east to west. Then the beetle would lay its eggs in the ball of dung and bury it. A month later it would dig up the ball and push it into the water and baby beetles would hatch. This east to west movement symbolized to the Egyptians the rising and setting of the sun hence the association to the solar gods.

Boar: The boar represents strength, fierceness and stubbornness. The snout and tusk symbolize fertility because of the phallic shape. One of the powers attributed to the boar is finding secret hidden things because of its rooting abilities. Mythology is filled with stories of swine with the power to absorb evil, negative energies.

Bull: The bull has been a long time symbol of fertility through sacrifice with its bringing nourishment through slaughter. The bull is the symbol of the sun. Bulls were worshipped in Egypt and Greece. The Egyptian God Osiris is often depicted with the head of a bull. In Greece comes the tales of a Minotaur. The astrological sign of the bull is the Taurus, a sign that deals with the earth and possessions. The bull links with the feminine through its horns is lunar crescent. The bull is associated with stubbornness, sowing seeds and rushing headlong into things.

Cat: Cats have always symbolized magic and mystery. They have been associated with curiosity, independence, and cleverness and healing. Old tales say a witch could take the form of a cat.

Throughout time humans have always feared the dark it represented the unknown and mystery. Cats can see very well in the dark therefore cats have been associated with mystery and magic.

Deer or Stag: The deer is the symbol of gentleness whereas the stag counters with power and strength. Deer have the power to bring new adventure into one's life, as Sir Gawain found out in following a hart in the King Arthur tales. The stag's antlers represent antenna which connects the male to higher levels of awareness and perception. Since they grow behind the eyes the antlers also symbolize the wildness within.

Dragons: When one thinks of magic, wizard and witches the medieval image of the dragon comes to mind. Dragons were creatures that embodied the power of the four elements. The dragon force to the druids was the primal abyss of the pre-progression of the earth itself. The power of the dragon and the four elements is related to different parts of the dragon. The breath of the dragon represented the element of air. The element of fire, through the dragon's fire breathing ability. The body of the dragon represented the element of Earth and the tail of the dragon represented water. The power

188

of the dragon was attributed to his ability to rule the sky and the earth.

Eagles: The symbol of the zenith of spirit, the thunderbird to Native Americans with its soaring flight ability the Eagle represented the power to rise above creation and connect with the divine. The eye sight of the Eagle was so powerful it represented the ability to have clear vision of past, present and future events therefore connecting it with divination.

Goat: Goats generally come from mountain areas. This is why they are seen as having the ability or attribute of seeking new heights in the higher realms. The goat is linked to the astrological sign of Capricorn honored so well that is was permanently affixed in the heavens. The goat is also connected to divination because of its horns. The curve symbolizes the ability to see what lies around the corner or in the future. The most famous goat god is Pan in Greek myths with his connection to the horn of plenty.

Horse: Mythology abounds with the horse. Odin in Norse legends rode an eight-legged steed. In Hindu, the chariot of the sun god is pulled by stallions as well as the chariot of Apollo in the Greek legends. The horse because it could be ridden and especially if it could fly like Pegasus is linked with the wind and clairvoyance in magic. Its power is movement, travel and freedom.

Lion: With the title of the king of the jungle the lion is naturally connected to royalty. In Egypt it was believed that the lion ruled the annual floods of the Nile. The male lion in a pride is a protector against predators. They use their roar to scare prey toward the lioness, which does most of the hunting. The lion is linked to the sun because it was believed it gave birth to new days.

Raven: The raven in myths represents birth, death and mysticism. From Edgar Allen Poe to the bible the raven has a wealth of lore about it. To the Celts it was sign of death and war. The Goddess Morrigu is called the Battle Raven. Odin was known to shape-shift into a raven. Its feathers being black and shiny linked it to the underworld. The raven was known as the messenger to the magician within. It teaches how to go into the dark and bring forth the light.

Snake: The snake represents rebirth, resurrection and wisdom. To the Native Americans it stands for healing and change. The Greeks also attributed the snake with healing properties. The God Hermes had a staff with entwined snakes upon it. The snake is also a symbol of sexual and creative energies. The Indian god Shiva wore snakes as bracelets and necklaces for sexuality. In Egypt the headband worn by the priests and priestesses known as the uraeus symbolized inner sight and control of the universe. This Egyptian headband always had a snake sticking out of it over the brow. The snake has no eyelids and its stare was said to mesmerize because it didn't blink. This is the mystical association given to the snake.

Gods with their animal associations:

Adonis (Greek): "Lord" the anointed one, god of love and beauty
> *Animal associations are: boar, doves and dogs*

Aegir (Norse): "Alebrewer" vanir god of the sea
> *Animal associations are: serpents and sea creatures*

Amon (Egypt): "great father," a phallic deity, god of fertility and agriculture
Animal associations are: the ram

Anubis (Egypt): "messenger of the gods, god of the underworld"
Animal associations are: the jackal and dogs

Ares (Greek): "god of war" blood thirsty and arrogant
Animal associations are: the ram relating to its golden fleece, the serpent

Bel (Irish): "son and fire god" connected to the Sabbat Beltaine
Animal associations are: all creatures of the forest

Bes (Egypt): "Lord of the land of Punt" a dwarf god of marriage and childbirth
Animal associations are: the leopard

Cernunnos (Celtic): "Antlered God of the Hunt" god of nature and forest
Animal associations are: stag, ram, bull and horned serpent

Dionysus (Greek): "Horned God" the bull headed god connected with pleasure, ecstasy and total abandon
Animal associations are: bull, stag and the ram

Enki (Sumerian): "Lord of Earth and primordial ocean"
Animal associations are: goat and all fish

El: (Canaanite): "Supreme God" master of time and a god of war
Animal associations are: the bull

Freyr: (Norse): "God of Yule" the lover; fertility god
Animal Associations are: the boar and the horse

Gwydion: (Welsh): "Wizard and bard of North Wales" a warrior-magician
Animal associations are: the white horse

Gwynn Ap Nudd: (Welsh): "King of Faeries and the underworld" leader of the wild hunt
Animal associations are: the stag and dogs

Horus: (Egypt): "Falcon-headed sky deity" the divine child
> *Animal associations are: falcons and cats*

Itzamna: (Mayan): "Sky God" omnipotent creator of humans
> *Animal associations are: the jaguar*

Khepri: (Egypt): "God of reincarnation and resurrection
> *Animal associations are: the scarab beetle*

Manannan MacLir: (Irish): "Shape shifter god of the sea and weather:
> *Animal associations are: sea creatures and the pig*

Marduk: (Babylonian): "Lord of life" ruler of the four quarters of the earth
> *Animal associations are: the bull calf*

Mars: (Roman): "God of spring, war and agriculture"
> *Animal associations are: woodpecker, horse and wolf*

Manu: (Egypt): "Lord of foreign lands" a fertility god
Animal associations are: the white bull

Mithras: (Persian): "A Sun God" all wise and all knowing
Animal associations are: the bear and bull

Nabu: (Sumerian): "Son of Marduk" god of writing and destiny
Animal associations are: the serpent headed dragon

Neptune: (Greek): "A sea God who ruled with a trident"
Animal associations are: horses and bulls

Odin: (Norse): "All Father" sky god, god of war and the wild hunt
Animal associations are: wolves, ravens and horses

Pan: (Greek): "Horned one of nature" horned and hoofed, little god
Animal associations are: goat and forest animals

Perun: (Slavic): "Lord of the universe" creator god, lord of thunder
> *Animal associations are: goat, cock, bear and bull*

Poseidon: (Greek): "Supreme Lord of the inner and outer oceans and seas"
> *Animal associations are: horse, bulls and all sea creatures*

Shiva: (Indian): "Lord of the World and Cosmic Dance"
> *Animal associations are: white bulls and elephants*

Svantovit: (Slavic): "God of the Gods" who had four heads
> *Animal associations are: the white horse*

Tekkeitsertok: (Inuit): "Most powerful god of the earth and hunting"
> *Animal associations are: deer*

Tezcathipcca: (Aztec): "The shadow; he who is at the shoulder"
> *Animal associations are: the jaguar*

Thor: (Norse): "God of thunder" champion of the gods
Animal associations are: goat

Tsai Shen: (Chinese): "God of Wealth"
Animal associations are: the cock and the carp

Vishnu: (Indian): "The preserver; lord of light, conqueror of darkness"
Animal associations are: the garuda bird, white horses, cobras and serpents

Zeus: (Greek): "Supreme God" lord of the heavens
animal associations are: the eagle

XVIII Epilogue

("Dogmatism" - positiveness in assertion of opinion especially when unwarranted or arrogant.)

There is a lot of social dogmatism in our culture and every culture worldwide, about what it means to be a man? Most experts attribute this dogmatism to patriarchal religions and their doctrines of an all powerful male deity. They may state that their God is conceived as being genderless; however all of their scriptural writings refer to their God as He or Him.

In their concepts, God created man first and woman was an afterthought and she is under subjection to the man. The subconscious programming derived within our English language is very interesting and may show how some of the old patriarchal concepts were interlaced into our culture. For instance, the word "female", the prefix "fe" has its roots in middle French meaning "property". The word "male" has its roots in the Latin homo, which means one and the same: alike; which later was associated with the word human with roots in the Latin humus, which means earth.

The English word, "man" has its roots in the Old English word "mon" which means human - humus, of the earth. The English word "woman" broken down to wo/man. As stated earlier, "man" means earth, the prefix "wo" has its roots in Latin as "vae", Old English as "wa" and in Middle English as "wo". In modern English it is "woe". Webster's definition of woe is, "a condition of deep suffering from misfortune, afflicton or grief."

From these examples of our language we can see how the subconscious programming has influenced our culture's concept of the female gender as being, woe unto man or woe unto the earth, and under subjection to the male gender and over the centuries has indoctrinated this dogmatism into our society.

The proof of this male chauvinistic attitude stemming from male dominant Religions are in the Judeo-Christian Bible which also coincides with the Muslim Quran. When God asked Adam why he ate from the tree to which he commanded him not to eat from, Adam wimped out and passed the buck and said, "The woman you put here with me- she gave me some fruit and I ate it." (Genesis 3:12) God then cursed Eve saying, "With pain you will give birth to children. Your desire will be for your husband and he will rule over you." (Genesis 3:16) "Then God cursed the ground, the earth." (Genesis 3:17), which he referred often to as She and Her.

After that, Adam still not taking responsibility for his own actions "Named his wife Eve because she would become the mother of all living." (Genesis 3:20) In other words, woman or the mother was the cause of all of humanities problems.

We can see how this patriarchal dogma has influenced the unconscious mind of humanity, for over five thousand years. We must all take into account that the religious writings of the Bible, Talmud and the Quran were written by men not women. One has to admit that this male dominating doctrine has crept into the subconscious and affects our culture, whether we follow those faiths or not. These concepts are deeply rooted in the collective unconscious.

Advances have been made in the last one hundred years with women's rights and powers. This however only forces men to acknowledge the individual rights of women on a secular constitutional level. It does not eliminate the biased or prejudiced attitudes about women in the world. With the emergence of the Wiccan and Pagan religions and their philosophies in the last fifty years, men now have the opportunity to educate themselves, about themselves.

There is no set of commandments in modern Wicca. There are no hardened rules of morality in modern paganism. This does not mean that

Wicca/Paganism is without ethical standards. Individual expression and freedom of choice are two qualities that are highly respected and promoted in the unwritten tenets of the religion. However, these qualities are not at the expense of encroaching upon another's rights of expression. Celebrating diversity is the motto of most Pagans.

Knowledge is one thing, practical application is another. The moral value system in the United States is in a sad state. The Presidents of our highest universities are on salaries of one to two hundred thousand dollars a year. These people are in charge of educating our next generation of young people. These young people are to eventually grow into positions of influence for our culture. The television and movie entertainers are making millions of dollars a year. This tells us something about the American people and their values. We, as Americans will pay ten times more to be entertained than they ever will to be educated.

Ethical practices in business in this country are also extremely corrupt. It seems the right thing to do morally does not apply to business, especially when it comes to profit and loss. We have accepted this standard as secularly correct. The statement of, I have ethics but they are situational is even true among Wiccans and Pagans.

It seems the qualities of chivalry are long gone and forgotten, even in the practice of modern Wicca and Paganism. The qualities of valor, justice, modesty, loyalty, courtesy and compassion used to be the ideal of what manhood was and a model for emulation.

There are many young Roves in our religion who are not practicing safe sex. Aside from the obvious venereal dangers how many have become fathers at a time in their lives when they were not ready for the Father stage. This is because they did not know or understand chivalry.

Wicca has been called a sexual religion that promotes infidelity. This may be due to new people coming into the craft trying to escape the authoritarian dogma of Christianity where sexual activity has been seen as forbidden between unmarried couples. Wicca has no such dogma.

While some Wiccans/Pagans practice sexual rites, in general sex is considered a sacred act. Casual sex stems from the creative urge or instinct also known as the sex drive. The act of sexual union itself sets up subtle forces that create a vortex that extends into the higher planes of existence. If the copulating couple have no spiritual higher plane contact, the vortex is powerful in the lower astral plane, however quite unbalanced in the other planes. When we fully understand these forces with which we work, and to a degree control, it creates responsibility. To ignore that responsibility and not put it into ethical practice in our lives is to dishonor ourselves and the Gods.

Another outlook on ethics is the Wiccan Rede, *"An It Harm None Do Thou What Thy Wilt."* This has been a running discussion between Wiccans and Pagans for many years.

First of all the Rede is not ancient script. It cannot be traced back any farther than Gerald Gardner, in "Witchcraft Today, 1954". There have been many different variations of it since its conception.

Secondly, the Rede is not a law or even a rule. It's a Rede. The meaning of the word Rede means advice or counsel. Therefore if anything it is a guideline for emulation. A statement for personal ethics. Much like we were taught as children in this society, "You do not start trouble, but you do not run from it either."

One version of the Rede reads, *"An in harm none, do thou what thy wilt, lest it be in self defense of thy life."* One could interpret this as defense of not only your physical life but your mental, emotional and spiritual life as well.

There is nothing in the Wiccan religion that says we have to stand there and take it, or turn the other cheek. We can defend ourselves as long as we are willing to accept the responsibility of our actions.

The old expression, "You've got to stand for something or you will fall for anything," relates to personal honor and integrity. Honor is a gift one gives to oneself and nobody can take it from you. It is a set of basic principles that one believes are right action. Standing and upholding those principles in one's life at any cost is integrity. This strengthens the spirit.

This is the backbone of the Wiccan religion; with the teachings of the old ways of honor and the integrity within the tenets of Paganism, gives the religion power and strength. This is the foundation for growth and guarantees its continuance through to the next generations.

It is the responsibility of the older generation of Sages and Fathers to pass these qualities on to the upcoming Roves. We need to promote the concept in these modern times, that to be of the Wiccan and Pagan faiths to be a part of… not necessarily better or happier, but different from the common humanity.

Pagan men need to know and understand themselves and their true nature. We are of the earth. The earth is our Mother. From Her we came and unto Her we must return. The God force within us is the ability to make change occur within Her manifestation.

One of the ways we are helping modern pagan men to relate to this God force is with our Brothers of the Sun gathering at the SDCW-ATC in August each year. Our hope is for the next generation of young men coming up in Paganism and Wicca, to make this knowledge and teaching available to them so they can teach and pass it on to future generations.

That is the main purpose of the SDCW-ATC *(Southern Delta Church of Wicca-ATC)* and why it was formed as a church. To be a place where solitary practitioners, groups and interested persons can come to learn, study and worship with like-minded people in the ways of the Old Religion.

While we do not proselytize, we do advertise our accessibility; to promote the tenets and studies of the religion of Wicca and Paganism to the general public.

To all of the modern Pagan men in the world today remember the words over the door at the Temple of Delphi, *"Know Thyself."*

IXX APPENDIX

The Eight Sabbats:

Winter Solstice December 21st

To most Wiccan- Pagan traditions this Sabbat represents the rebirth of the Sun God for the new solar year. It is a solar festival and celebrated with fire. The Sun God at Winter Solstice represents the divine child of promise who will bring back warmth to the earth from the dead of winter.

The Yule log is an ancient tradition and its burning symbolizes the fire of the new born Sun King. The log is dressed and decorated with sprigs of holly to represent the Holly King of the dying year making way for the Oak King of the New Year.

The tradition of decorating a Yule tree is an old Pagan custom similar in meaning to the burning of the Yule log. The earliest record of a decorated Yule tree was in 1510 in Latuia. It was danced around in the Market place then set on fire.

Imbolc (Imbolg) February 1st

As the sun waxes the days grow slowly longer. The Sabbat of Imbolg focuses on the waking up of the earth from its winter sleep. This is the time when the sap begins to run in the trees. A time when the first lambs and ewes are born. In fact the word Imbolc is old Gaelic for "In Milk".

One of the rituals performed at Imbolc is Bride's Bed. The last bundle of grain from last years harvest is kept and made into a grain dolly. It was believed years go that the Goddess stayed in the last grain harvested. Within the dolly she is to be the seed for the next harvest. During the ritual, the dolly is placed in a small bed and everyone chants around it to bring fertility to next year's crop. The chant is something like:

> *Blessed be the Bride*
> *Blessed be the Great Mother*

Since it is a festival of lights, candles are then lit to represent the waxing sun.

Spring Equinox March 21st

At this Sabbat, seed planting is at hand, not only physically but in the psychic planes as well. Seeds of wisdom, understanding, or magical skills are planted in the subconscious mind during rituals.

During spring rituals eggs are utilized because of the symbolism of the egg itself. The yellow yolk represents the Sun God and the white shell, the Goddess of the moon. The whole egg itself represents rebirth.

The vernal equinox is a time of balance between light and dark. A time to put winter behind us and look forward to the bright months ahead.

Beltaine May 1st

Beltaine celebrates the union of the God and Goddess. It is a fertility festival. With nature in full bloom and the Beltaine Fire lit it is a time for festivities.

One of the best well known traditions of Beltaine is the May Pole dance. Men and women gather around the pole with red and white ribbons attached to the top. The red ribbon symbolizes the menstrual blood of the Goddess. The white ribbon symbolizes the semen of the God. The pole itself is of course, a phallic symbol. Men and women dance around the pole wrapping the ribbons as they dance, magically producing fertility for the land and its people.

Summer Solstice June 21st

This mid summer Sabbat recognizes the sun at its peak of power along with it being the longest day of the year. It is also the time that begins the dark half of the year. Some traditions celebrate with the mock battle of the Oak King and Holly King. As the Oak King relinquishes his power to the Holly King, who will rule till Winter Solstice.

Another symbol used at the solstice ritual is the Sun Wheel or disc. The Sun Wheel represents the eight spoke Wheel of the Year. It is usually hung above the altar as a Talisman for blessing in the coming year.

Lughnasadh August 1st
This Sabbat honors the first harvest. It is a time when the first crops of grains fruits and vegetables are ripened. The baking of bread and cakes are sacred to this solar ritual. Bread represents the Lord of the Harvest, sacrificing his life under the sickle to sustain life. Sometimes the spirit of the grain is invoked into the loaf. This Sabbat celebrates and honors the God of Death and Resurrection.

Autumn Equinox/ Mabon Sept 21st
Known as the second harvest a time when nuts and berries are gathered. It is also the ripening of the grapes; a time for wine making. At Mabon, the night and day are equal, but the waning of the sun's power is also recognized. This is also the time to gather the last of the grain to be used in Bride's Bed at Imbolc in February. The Mabon Alters are decorated with nuts, berries, and herbs.

Samhain Oct 31st

This Sabbat honors the death of the Sun God, following the cycle of the year,
who will once again be reborn at Yule. Samhain is known as the third harvest festival. It also marks the beginning of the New Year. Some traditions honor this time with a Feast of the Dead or Dumb Supper.
The time of Samhain is when the veil between this realm and the next is at its thinnest. Communication with spirits and loved ones, who have crossed over, is more accessible on this night. Many celebrations utilize acts of divination as part of the ritual. In many traditions the Crones and Sages are honored at this Sabbat.

The Esbats: The Esbats are the Lunar Rites observed through worship, by most Wiccan/Pagan traditions. They are the New, Full, and Dark moon rituals. Where the Solar Rites are generally observed through celebration, the Esbats are usually celebrated by works of Magic. This is not to say that Magic cannot be worked during a Sabbat, on the contrary Solar Rites are a powerful time to work Magic. The Lunar Rites, since they occur more frequently, offer more times of availability to utilize the power of the moon for magical work.

As stated earlier, the moon is feminine and represents the Goddess. This is primarily due to the correlation between the cycle of the moon and the menstruation of women, both being twenty-eight days. Other factors are considered as well, such as the moon sitting in the black sky. allegorically it coincides with the story of the Goddess Diana being the darkness and her consort being the light; and out of the darkness came the light.

One can imagine that at sometime in history mankind looked up into the starry night and stared at the bright full moon. They gleamed at it with awe inspiring humbleness. As they stood there, they probably slipped into an altered state of consciousness. A soothing, calming, receptive mode. During that moment, early man might have opened up their awareness and felt, for just that moment, an oneness with the earth and the cosmos.

That feeling of security and contentment might have touched a subconscious memory of being in the womb, from which they came. So the related this feeling from the moon with the mother. This is the essence of the Lunar Rites in Wicca and Paganism we are presenting, for reference the mechanics of casting the circle, erecting the temple, and closing the circle, within a New Moon ritual. The ritual was written for a solitary practitioner.

NEW MOON RITUAL: In creating any ritual it is necessary to consider Sacred Space. Sacred Space in most of modern Wicca is the area that the ritual will be performed in. This could be in a house, in the forest, wherever a witch decides to cast their circle.

The area that the ritual is to be performed in has to be cleansed and consecrated to make it a Sacred Place. A place where mortals can commune with their Gods. This process is called erecting a temple.
One needs to understand that from the very moment a witch begins to think of a ritual and as they gather their tools and ready the sacred place, they are already beginning to work the Magick. *Sacred space becomes a place that is not a place, in a time that is not a time, in a world that is not a world.*

The items needed for this New Moon ritual are:
The pentacle
The athame or sword
The wand or staff
The cauldron or chalice
Also upon the altar you will need a God and Goddess representation. This could be as simple as two different colored candles. You will also need something to burn

for incense. And a small bowl of salt and a small bowl of water.

The circle needs to be marked on the ground or upon the floor so that the barriers of the edge of the circle are distinguishable. This can be a piece of rope or cord laid along the perimeter of the circle. You will also need representations in the four directions for the four elements. This could be also colored candles.

Now you are ready to begin your New Moon Rite. To cast he circle take the projective tool f either the athame or sword and walk clockwise to the northern quadroon of the circle. In some traditions the begin casting the circle in the East. The association is that in the spell of making the Magic begins in the element of AIR. Another way of looking at it is, since you are working Magic you are going to make change occur in the world which you already exist, therefore you have to begin casting the circle in the North at the element of Earth, to begin the transformation of the Sacred Circle. Either way is correct, it depends on which way feels right to you.

Now take the sword or athame and point it toward the ground in either the North or east quadrant. Visualize in your mind a stream of energy, of either white light or blue flame coming down from the ether and through the top of your head flowing down your arms and out of the Magical tool. As you begin walking clockwise imagine this stream of energy leaving a trail of either white light or blue flame as you walk around the circle.

As you walk say *"I conjure thee oh circle of power to manifest in this realm let it be a place where I may commune and join with he Gods."* Make sure as you are walking and speaking that you are timing is such as to end your speech as you complete the circle back to the original starting point. Now your circle is cast.

Now walk back to your alter and with the athame place the point of the knife in the bowl of salt and say *"I consecrate the O' Creature of Earth and make thee worthy to bee in this sacred circle."* Next, place the point of the athame in the bowl of water and say*" I cleanse thee O Creature of Water and make thee worthy to be in this sacred circle."* Next take three pinches of salt and drop them in the bowl of water. Then pick up the bowl and walk to the quadroon where you began casting the circle.

Walk the circle again while sprinkling drops of water on the ground or floor and say *"With the waters of life I no cleanse this sacred space, I banish all negativity and bane fullness from this place. By the power of the Old Ones, SO MOTE IT BE"!* Then walk back to the alter and pick up your incense and once again walk the circle holding the incense and say, " *With Fire and Smoke, I now consecrate this sacred space and make it worthy of a meeting place between mortals and their Gods"*.

Now that your temple is erected you call and summon the elements to assist in the power of the circle. Walking clockwise once again start in the North. Raise your hands as in praise, close your eyes and say *"Spirits of the north, element of earth, I summon thee to attend this sacred rite. I charge thee, by the power of the Old Ones. SO MOTE IT BE!!* With your eyes still shut, visualize a green mist swirling around the northern quadrant gathering at the edge of the circle.

Still walking clockwise, move to the eastern quadrant, raise your hands in praise and close your eyes again and say *"Spirits of the east, element of AIR, I summon thee to attend this sacred rite, I charge the by the powers of the Old Ones. SO MOTE IT BE!"* Now visualize a yellow mist swirling and gathering at the edge of the circle.

Moving to the southern quadrant, Raise your hands once again closing your eyes and say *"Sprits of the south element of Fire, I summon thee to attend this sacred rite. I charge thee by the power of the Old Ones. SO MOTE IT BE!"* Visualize a red mist swirling

216

and gathering at the edge of the circle.

Walk to the western quadrant, raise your hands, close your eyes and say *"Spirits of the west, element of Water, I summon thee to attend this sacred rite. I charge thee by the power of the Old Ones. SO MOTE IT BE!"* Visualize a blue mist swirling and gathering at the edge of the circle. From there move back to your alter.

Since it is a solitary practice, you invoke the Lord and the Lady. Starting with the invocation to the Goddess. Stand with your feet shoulder length apart, raise your hands in praise and say: *"I now invoke the Goddess of the Waxing Moon, let thy receptive energy fill this sacred space. Mistress of the hunt I call to you. Matrix of creation, I invoke you. SO MOTE IT BE!"*

Then for the invocation of the God stand with your feet shoulder length apart, raise your hands and say *"O great God of change and transformation I call thy essence down. Lord of life, death and resurrection. I invoke thee. Let thy energy and presence fill this sacred place. SO MOTE IT BE!"*

At this point in the ritual is when the statement of purpose is spoken. The intent and desire of Magic that is to be worked should now be clearly stated.

Building up magical power can be achieved in several ways, by dancing, chanting, singing, running whichever way suits you best. While the power is being built concentrate your mind on the end result of your desire. When you feel the peak of power, this will be sensed in the feeling, as if you are going to explode, at that point stop and drop to the ground or the floor and release the power that you have raised into the cosmos.

After a few minutes of rest, stand and raise your hands and say " *I thank thee O God of transformation for attending this sacred rite and lending thy energy to my Magic till such a time as I call on you again go in strength and go in power. SO MOTE IT BE!"* With your hands still raised now say *"I thank thee O goddess of the Moon for attending this sacred rite and accepting the seed of manifestation. till such a time that I call on you again. Go in peace and go in love. SO MOTE IT BE!"*

Now walking counterclockwise, move to the quadrant of the last element you invoked, we will start in water. Raise your hands in praise and say *"Spirits of the west, element of water, I thank thee for witnessing this sacred rite and lending thy energies to my Magic. Go now in strength and go in power. SO MOTE IT BE!"* Move to the southern quadrant, raise your hands in praise and say *"Spirits of the south element of fire I thank thee for witnessing this sacred rite and lending thy energies to my magic. GO in strength and go in power. SO MOTE IT BE!"*

Still moving counterclockwise within the circle, go to the eastern quadrant raise your hands in praise and say *"spirits of the east, elements of air, I thank thee for attending this sacred rite and lending thy energies to my magic. Go in strength and go in power. SO MOTE IT BE!"* Moving to the northern quadrant, raise your hands in praise and say *"spirits of the north, element of earth, I thank thee for attending this sacred rite and lending thy energies to my magic. Go in strength and go in power. SO MOTE IT BE!"*

Now with the magical tool you utilized in casting the circle start in the quadrant in the circle where you began casting. We will begin in north. Point the athame or sword toward the ground or floor and begin walking counterclockwise the perimeter of the circle. As you are walking visualize the blue flame or the white light of the circle being drawn back up into the athame or sword and flowing up your arm and out the top of your head back into the ether. While you are walking and visualizing you are saying "I now banish this magic circle, I widdershins the energies of this sacred space and it now becomes a place that is a place, in a time that is a time in a world that is a world. As you reach the starting point of the circle you state the circle is no more.

Color Correspondences: Color can be very important when working magic. It can be added to spells, rituals, and ceremonies to help make your intent known to the Gods. Here are the colors and their associations that are standard in Modern Paganism.

Red... Fire, South, Courage, Strength, Sexual Potency, Blood.

Pink... Love, Affection, Romance, Union of the male and female.

Yellow... Intellect, East, Mental Powers, Faults, Air.

Orange... Control, Stimulation, Adaptation, Attraction.

Green... Wealth, Money, Fertility, Earth, North, Health.

Blue... Truth, Wisdom, Water, West, Occult Power.

Purple... Psychic Powers, Divination, Spirit Contact.

Brown... Intuition, ESP, Study, Grounding.

Black... Dark Mother/Father, Reversing, Binding, Elimination.

White... Wholeness, the Moon, Semen of the God.

Silver... Victory, Meditation, Goddess Powers.

Gold... Understanding, Fast Luck, God Powers.

Planetary Associations:

Sun.. Jobs, Healing, Leadership, Projective Energy.

Moon.. Growth, Dreams, Divination, Receptive Energy.

Mars.. War, Lustfulness, Courage, Hunting.

Mercury.. Intelligence, Powers of the Mind, Communication.

Jupiter.. Luck, Money, Mundane Prosperity.

Venus.. Love, Pleasure, The Arts, Beauty.

Saturn.. Death, Transition, Reincarnation, Divorce.

Moons of the Months

January.. Wolf Moon
February.. Storm Moon
March.. Chaste Moon
April.. Seed Moon
May.. Hare Moon
June.. Partner Moon
July.. Mead Moon
August.. Wart Moon
September.. Barley Moon
October.. Blood Moon
November.. Snow Moon
December.. Oak Moon

Candle Magick:

When working candle magick it is useful to anoint the candle with oil. This can be olive oil or to give more intent to the magic the oil can be essential oil. Essential oils are infused with certain herbs so the magical properties of the herbs are blended with the oil. Here is a small list of herbs that are useful in different types of magic and are often infused in essential oils.

Herbs for Candle Magic:

Divination: Frankincense, Goldenrod, Mugwort, Wormwood.
Virility: Mandrake, Catnip, Ginseng, Myrtle.
Health: Allspice, Feverfew, John the Conqueror, Peppermint.
Love: Basil, Burdock, Columbine, Dragon's Blood.
Money: Cinnamon, Honeysuckle, Skullcap, Vervain.
Protection: Aaron's rod, Angelica, Coltsfoot, Mistletoe.

The first step in candle magic is to choose a candle of the appropriate color (refer to the Color correspondence chart) that relates to the intent or purpose of the spell work. The subconscious does not recognize words; therefore the color of the candle symbolizes the desire or result of the magical intent of the magician. To anoint a candle take some oil in the palm of your hand and roll the candle between the hands, starting at the bottom of the candle and working towards the top. This is planting the desire in the base of the candle and channeling the energy upwards towards the wick where the flame can carry the magic into the ether.

It also adds power to use an incantation while anointing the candle. An incantation is using words or song to influence the charm or spell. Here is an example of an incantation for anointing a candle.

"I consecrate and bless this candle
By the powers of the old gods
As the flame does burn so shall my desire
Thus combined my will is done"

At this point the candle is set in a holder and a meditation is performed. The desire or purpose of the spell is fully visualized in as much detail as possible. It is important to see the finished product or desire completed as if it already existed. Emotions need to be added to the vision to be brought up and actually felt while doing the meditation.

This part of the spell should not be rushed. Take as much time as necessary to crystallize the image. When the meditation is done, light the candle and chant an incantation over the flame. This is to raise added energy to the work. Repeat the chant several times and feel the energy burn through the flame and expand into the cosmos. When this is completed and you no longer can retain the image continuously, the spell is done. Let the candle burn out so that it continues the magic until it is spent.

Candle Magic Invocations:

General Chants:
"With smoke and flame and candle glow
I release the magic and let it go
With the power of moon and sun
This spell hath begun"
"By incantation and sacred song
I call to make my magic strong
Earth, Air, Water, and Fire
Work ye now unto my desire"

For Money:
"Magick blend and candle burn
Money is mine at every turn"

For Health:
"I cast away baneful ill
By the power of my will
With courage and might
I call this down tonight"

For Love:
"Once, Twice, Thrice around
Love shall abound
By choice and will it shall be free
Draw the one that's meant for me"

For Protection:
"Upon the powers I do implore
Shields of strength of ancient lore
Protection I call all around me
This is my will so mote it be"

MAGICAL GLOSSARY

Atom: One of the minute particles of which according to ancient materialism the universe is composed. Considered the source of vast potential energy.

Bacchus: The Greek god of wine and infidelity, from which the English word Bachelor is derived.

Consciousness: The quality or state of being aware of something within oneself. The upper level of mental life of which the person is aware of sensation, emotion, volition and thought.

Baneful: Product of destruction; something that causes serious harm. The word was generally implied with poisons.

Clergy: A group of people ordained to perform the sacerdotal functions of a church or religious faith.

Chant: A rhythmic monotonous utterance of words or song used in the working of magic or to sing praise of celebration.

Cosmic Law: The systematic order of energy transmutation that exists; according to the examination of science in the entire cosmos.

Crone: one of the triple aspects of the Goddess. Also an esteemed title of life given to elder women in the Wiccan religion. A woman who is wise and experienced.

Dark Magick: A type of energy work where negative attributes are examined and usually forced under control or eliminated.

Elements: the powers or forces utilized by magicians to enact change in the realms. They are seen as the four active forces of creation in the physical expressions of earth, air, fire and water.

Esbats: The lunar rites or liturgy performed at different moon phases known as new moon, full moon and dark moon rituals.

Incantations: The use of verbal charms spoken or sung in rituals of magick. A formula of words designed to produce a particular effect.

Instinct: A largely inheritable and unalterable tendency of an organism to respond to environmental stimuli without involving reason. Behavior mediated by reactions below the conscious level.

Maiden: One of the aspects of the triple goddess. In women an age of life before motherhood. A woman who is unattached, not married or handfasted.

Magick: The influenced manipulation of energies to bring about a desired outcome or effect, according to the will of the magician. Spelled with a final k to distinguish it from stage magic or illusion.

Magic Circle: An area designed to perform magic in. A circle of various sizes and circumference, cleansed consecrated and dedicated to a magical purpose.

Magic Tools: The implements used by a magician, witch or Wiccan in the performance of magic.

Pagan: The term comes from Latin which means country dweller. Today it represents any group of religions that are basically non-Christian oriented and are classified as nature based.

Power: The ability to act or produce an effect. Having the capacity for being acted upon or undergoing an effect. Power implies possession of ability to wield force.

Priest/Priestess: A man or woman who has the ability to dispense sacraments in a religious ceremony.

Psychic Energy: A level of energy that is immaterial or spiritual in origin. Marked by extraordinary or mysterious sensitivity, perception or understanding.

Psychology: The study of mind and behavior in relation to a particular field of knowledge or activity. The science of mind and behavior.

Rites: A pre-described form of words and actions of a ceremony. The liturgy of a church of coven. A ceremonial act or actions such as initiations.

Rove: One of the triple aspects of the God. In men it is a time of life when the man is unattached, not married or Handfasted.

Sabbat: Celebration honoring the solar cycle of the year. There are eight times in the year when Wiccans witches and pagans celebrate and honor the God and the seasonal, agricultural times of the year.

Sage: One of the triple aspects of the God. In men the term signifies a man who has attained eldership in his life. A man who is wise in experience.

Trance: A state of partially suspended animation. An altered state of consciousness below normal waking awareness.

Wicca: A modern religion that has its roots dating back to the nineteen-fifties. Its followers utilize the mythology of European cultures. Wiccan rituals and practices are believed to partially descend from ancient traditions.

Witchcraft: A religious practice of magic dating back approximately three hundred years. It is associated with Wicca in its practice and application.

BIBLIOGRAPHY

"My Road to the Sundance", by Manny Two Feathers, Wo-Pila Publishing, Erie PA 1994.

"The Golden Bough", by James G. Frazer, Gramercy Books, New York NY.

"Celtic Myths and Legends", by Charles Squire, Gramercy Books, New York NY 1994.

"The White Goddess", by Robert Graves, The Noonday Press, New York NY 1948.

"Mark of Voodoo", by Sharon Caulder Ph.D., Llewellyn Publications, 2002.

"Wicca for Men", by A. J. Drew, Carol Publishing Group, 1998.

"Wiccan Warrior", by Kerr Cuhulain, Llewellyn Publications, 2000.

"People of the Earth", by Ellen Evert Hopman, Destiny Books, Rochester Vermont 1996.

"West Country Wicca", by Rhiannon Ryall, Phoenix
Publishing Inc., 1989.

"There is a River, The Story of Edgar Cayce", by
Thomas Sugrue, Are. Press, Association for Research
and Enlightenment Inc., Virginia Beach VA 1973.

"The Sacred Cauldron, Secrets of the Druids", by
Tadhg MacCrossan, Llewellyn Publications 1992.

"Twenty Years A-Growing", by Maurice O'Sullivan,
Oxford University Press 1977.

"The Witch's Way", by Janet and Stewart Farrar,
Phoenix Publishing Inc. 1984.

"An ABC of Witchcraft", by Doreen Valiente, Phoenix
Publishing Inc. 1973.

"Deepening Witchcraft", by Greycat, ECW Press,
Toronto, Ontario, Canada 2002.

"The Alex Sanders Lectures", by Alex Sanders,
Magickal Childe Publishing Inc. 1984.

"The Book of Merlin", by R. J. Stewart, Sterling Publishing Co. Inc. New York NY 1987.

"Essentials of Psychology", by Dennis Coon, Seventh Edition, Brooks/Cole Publishing Co.1997.

"Experimental Methods in Psychology", by Robert C. Calfee, CBS College Publishing, New York NY 1985.

"Sociology, Sixth Edition", by John J. Macionis, Simon and Schuster/A Viacom Company, New Jersey 1997.

"Psychology and Life", Fourteenth Edition, by Philip G. Zimbardo and Richard J. Gerrig,
Harper Collings College Publishers, New York NY 1996.

"Pagans and Christians", by Robin Lane Fox, Alfred A. Knopf Inc. 1986.

"The Warrior as Healer", by Thomas R. Joiner, Healing Arts Press, Rochester Vermont 1999.

"The Mabinogi", by Patrick K. Ford, University of California Press 1977.

"Classical Mythology", by Mark Morford and Robert Lenardon, Longman Inc., New York and London 1977.

"Lord of Light and Shadow", by D. J. Conway, Llewellyn Publications 1997.

"Druidcraft", by Philip Carr-Gromm, Published by Thorsons 2002.

"Complete Book of Witchcraft", by Raymond Buckland, Llewellyn Publications 1997.

"God is Red", by Vine DeLoria Jr., Fulcrum Publishing, Golden CO 1992.

"Personality Plus", by Florence Littahuer, Published by Fleming H. Revell 1983.

"Witchcraft Today, The Modern Craft Movement," Edited by Chas S. Clifton, Llewellyn Publications 1992 .

"The Celts", Nora Chadwick, Penguin Books, Middlesex England, 1979.

"The Magic of Believing", Claude Bristol, Pocket Books, New York, 1969.

"The Age of Chivalry, Bullfinch's Mythology", Doubleday Books and Music Clubs Inc., New York, 1995.

"Bio-rhythm", Bernard Gittelson, Warner Books, New York, 1975.

"Anthropology of Folk Religion", Charles Leslie, Vintage Books, New York, 1960.

Rev. Terry Michael Riley is the founding High Priest of the Southern Delta Church of Wicca – A.T.C. in Jonesboro, Arkansas, established in 1994. He was ordained by the Aquarian Tabernacle Church in 1993. He is a respected sage in his Pagan community. He has been teaching men's mysteries in the craft through workshops, classes and open festivals for the past sixteen years. He is a healer and teacher.

Since 1995 Terry has performed over 180 Rites of Passage for the Pagan community in his tri-state area.

241